CW01669852

THE CASTLE

Alex was right. The rippers came back. But it wasn't a rip-off, or even an attack. It was a massacre. The house was dark. The outside spotlights were off. Jeff and Alex were in the attic, with Deb and Kristy; the attic windows, nearly thirty feet above the ground, commanded excellent views on both sides of the house. The others waited in the darkened house downstairs, all armed and ready behind double-barred doors and the iron window screens. There was more tension in the house, Scott had said, than there was in the power lines. His father had remarked the remark. It was the kind of thing that came from minds that were trying to be writers, and once Scott got all that old Poe-type imagery out of his head he might be the writer in the family yet. Jeff was at the northwest window, the one that looked down the long steep hill to the big road. The road was plainly marked by its luminous center- and side-stripes. What he had seen was a damsight closer, just over the hill, just below the cesspool. He squinted. The peachtree trembled, and he swept his gaze back and forth, but nothing else was moving. There was no breeze.

Then he heard the sound of a throat's being cleared, and a moment later moonlight glinted on metal: a gun barrel . . .

Also by Andrew J. Offutt
and in Magnum Books

MESSENGER OF ZHUVASTOU

ANDREW J. OFFUTT

The Castle Keeps

MAGNUM BOOKS
Methuen Paperbacks Ltd.

A Magnum Book

THE CASTLE KEEPS
ISBN 0 417 02150 X

First published 1972
by Berkley Medallion Books, Inc, New York
Magnum edition published 1978

Magnum Books are published
by Methuen Paperbacks Ltd
11 New Fetter Lane, London EC4P 4EE

Set in Linotype Times

Made and printed in Great Britain
by Hazell Watson & Viney Ltd,
Aylesbury, Bucks

To Jodie, until further notice

The writer wishes to express his thanks to
Robert Ardrey of *The Territorial Imperative*
Desmond Morris of *The Naked Ape* and
Garrett de Bell *et al.* of *The Environmental Handbook,*

who helped so much with this story and whom he has never met; and to all the nice old gentlemen in Washington, who have obviously never heard of any of the above.

Chapter One

'Dad.'

Jeff Andrews turned, lifting his eyebrows a little. His son's voice, from the other side of a low-drooping redbud flanked by three big maples, was quiet. Calling him.

'Yeah.'

'We had company last night.'

Jeff Andrews' hand dropped to his holstered revolver, touched it fleetingly, came back up to shift his rifle into a two-handed grip. He waited. Andy said nothing else. A catbird scrawked its ugly noise, stilling the cardinals and towhees and juncos for a moment. Then they went on with their happy conversation, Catbirds were a rude lot, but they were sometimes valuable as sentinels.

Using the barrel of his rifle, Jeff wiped aside the leafy switches of buckbush and waded through. He ducked under the tired Judas tree. Turned almost sidewise to pass between a sapling and a fat old buckeye. Stepped around the big maple.

Andy glanced his way, then returned his gaze to what he'd found.

He was a tall boy, looked like he was going to be taller. Maybe two or three more inches; already his height matched his father's six feet plus a quarter-inch, and he could no longer wear Jeff's socks. Kids' feet kept getting bigger, generation after generation. Jeff's grandfather had had dainty little size 6-A's. Jeff's father had worn size 8-1/2. Jeff had been able to wear them for exactly seven months, during his fifteenth year, before his feet were bigger than his dad's. Now Granpod and Jeff senior were both fertilizing the soil, and Jeff wasn't Jeff Junior anymore, and he wore a size 10-1/2-C shoe and already his older son's feet were bigger, and now that son had found the body of a man.

They stood side by side, looking down at him. Or it;

once a man is beyond EKG and EEG he passes into itdom; he is the body, the remains, it.

It wore a pair of denims and with reinforced stitching and brass studs on the pockets. It wore a dark jacket, shiny nylon or something, resembling an Air Force flight jacket. And it wore a red baseball cap, and a holstered pistol. Its hand was still wrapped around its .30-06, index finger inside the trigger guard.

'Well,' Jeff Andrews said.

'Yeah,' Andy Andrews said.

'Not too damned pretty, is it, son?'

'No sir. Not too damned. But he'd have been a lot uglier if he'd made it to the house.'

'And a lot more trouble.'

Andy nodded. 'And a lot more trouble. So – whadda we do with him?'

Jeff glanced around, stepped closer to the maple and leaned his rifle against it. He put his hands into his pockets and came out with tobacco and papers. Andy watched him roll the cigaret, lick it and twist both ends, and push it into his mouth. All the while gazing blank-faced down at the dead man. He took out a kitchen match, snapped it aflame with his fingernail, and lit up. His cheeks sank in as he pulled at the cigaret, meanwhile shaking out the match. Holding the cigaret in the same hand with the match, he moistened the thumb and forefinger of his other hand and squeezed the black matchtip. Then he dropped the dead match beside the dead man.

'Recycle,' he told the little white stick with its black head, and he stepped on it to push it down into the soil.

Andy waited. He had asked a question; his father had heard. It wasn't a question he would ignore. But first there was the almost-ritual with the cigaret, handmade in government-approved No-Tar papers. Andy didn't smoke, for two simple reasons, although he was more aware of the second than of the first, which he would better understand as he grew older.

The first reason was that his father had told him, more than once, that he could smoke any time he wanted, although it wasn't too damned bright, and please ask me, son, for the makin's, so when you get sick I'll know right away what caused it. Subtle, clever. Andy thus had no reason to sneak-smoke, which was how his father and most of his generation and the generations before that had begun, male and female alike. Too, the simple little cause-effect suggestion had been put into his mind. You smoke, you're going to get sick. So he hadn't. He wasn't too wild about the smell, either.

The second reason was that Andy simply thought the habit was a pretty dumb one, government-approved/guaranteed tarless paper or not. And it certainly wasn't ecological. Tobacco plants made better fertilizer than ashes, any day. As for tobacco *stalks* – they were so rich people still strewed them on their lawns, when they had lawns. City people rich enough to have yards paid ridiculous sums for them.

Andy wondered if the dead man was from a city. Probably. They usually were. People around here knew better than to go wandering at night, except in the areas they had all agreed were to be left alone, with their trees. That way there would still be birds and rabbits and squirrels and possums. No, this fellow was probably from a city, certainly from Off, and not hunting animals, either. He'd been coming up on their hill.

Andy's chin came up; he glanced quickly about.

His father smiled at him. It was that tolerant little smirk that you couldn't really like. It was superior, and Jeff knew it, but he had never been able to conquer it.

'No,' he said. 'If he'da had company they'da taken him with them. Or we'd have heard from them.'

'Um hmm.' His father had answered his unspoken question. His sudden realization and automatic looking around; this dead man might not have been alone. But the first question remained unanswered, while Jeff Andrews smoked and stood gazing down at the corpse.

He squatted to make elaborately certain the butt was dead, grinding it and touching the tip several times with a wetted forefinger. Then he shoved his hand into his denim jacket – which he wore over nothing today, it was that warm – and pulled out his rubber gloves. They made rubbery, squeegy noises as he pulled them on. He glanced at Andy.

'I think we better take him home.'

Andy refrained from making a face. 'I hope we get to draw or something for who buries him.'

Jeff looked back at the corpse, stony-faced. 'I will. In several places. We can use him.'

'Ugh,' Andy said, and added, 'recycle.'

'Yeah. Dust you were, to dust return. So we put them in boxes that prevented them from returning to dust, to fertilize the soil. Still . . . there's always been a little seepage, or somethin'. Used to be a prime subject of newspaper editorials, all the weeds in graveyards. Lord, why not? Most fertile land in the coun – you know what a graveyard is?'

'Sure.'

'Um. Occurs to me you've never heard the word. First it was cemeteries. Then when that got popular, it got to be memorial gardens. No one ever said graveyards. Or dead, either. Passed on and passed over, or was "called". And the deceased.' Same as "fuck", he thought. That got so popular a few years ago we had to come up with another one. So now it's "sink".

'*You* say graveyards,' Andy pointed out.

'Oh. Stand back.'

Jeff rose, bent and laid hold of the man's shoulders with his rubber-gloved hand. He grunted, then moved his feet farther apart.

'Been here awhile,' he said.

'Need help?'

'Gotny rubber gloves?'

'Nosir.'

'Stand back. Uh!' He strained. He moved his feet in closer, careful not to touch the body. He heaved. The dead man came up, limp and loose and looking as if he weighed ninety tons. Jeff half-spun and lurched; the corpse's arms flailed as it swung and sprawled loosely like a half-empty bag of rotting potatoes. Jeff blew out his cheeks, gazing a moment at the body. It was still – or rather again – face down.

He squatted to examine the electrified wire that had killed the man who had tried to intrude, carrying two guns, on his property. He looked up, his mouth opening to speak, but Andy was already scooping up a double handful of leaves, dropping them at his father's side, scooping more.

Carefully, Jeff reconcealed the wire. He rose to inspect it, bent to flick away a leaf that had come from too deep, and turned to look at the body.

Andy stood beside it. 'Want to see his face?'

'No. I can wait.'

'Shall we take 'im back now?'

'No. He can wait, too. Let's go ahead and complete the circuit. We'll come back for 'im – it's not all that far.'

They covered the other wire, then left the body, walking side by side around the edge of the tree-covered hill. The camouflaged electric wire running along the ground beneath the leaves and grass and trailing undergrowth was undisturbed.

'Dad?'

'Yeah?'

'What if you and Mom *had* gone to Australia?'

Jeff shrugged. 'It was just a dream. Just something we talked about with the Andersons and some others. We mighta been serious, all of us, if something had really catalyzed us. Nothing did. Everybody had dreams. There was a time I considered going to Ireland, too. Funny about that; your mother was ready, I think. They had this thing about tax breaks for artists. Creators in the arts, writers, painters, all of it, I think. But we didn't do that either. We just talked about it.'

'Did you ever write to anyone in Australia, Dad? The State Department, or whatever they have?'

Jeff shook his head. 'They were wailing for immigrants then, too. All you had to do was develop some land, but of course that wasn't my thing. I was raised on a farm, and I had enough of it. Writing for a living isn't like anything else. Writing's a hobby, and when you get paid for doing your hobby . . . well, you sure don't want to have to go to work.' Jeff smiled. How many times he'd said that! How long since the last lecture?

Walking back along the line to where the dead man waited, Jeff didn't even smile.

'And now it's *really* an island,' Andy said, rather wistfully. 'With a mile-high KEEP OUT sign. Harbors and coastlines bristling with gunnery.'

'Makes sense, son. That's what we are. An island. And this hill bristles, as you put it, with gunnery.' He hefted the rifle, nodded at Andy's, touched the butt of his pistol.

'And electric,' Andy said. They were walking up to the sprawled man, now. He still clutched his rifle.

'Yeah.' Jeff squatted beside the man, turned him over. 'Uh!'

Ugly. Wide, bright eyes. Very surprised. That one last, big, final surprise as he came down on enough voltage to electrocute an elephant – had there been any elephants. Shielded; no possibility of fire, no matter how many men stepped on it or how long this one lay here.

Andy stared, fascinated; Jeff closed the man's eyes. That helped. The wide-frozen mouth, though, wouldn't close. Jeff unbuckled his holster belt, which wasn't easy. He slipped it off the man, handed it back to Andy.

'Uh—'

'He doesn't need it anymore, son.' Jeff didn't look around. After a moment leather creaked as Andy strapped the belt on. Except that it wasn't leather, of course. Practically nothing was; everything seemed to be plastic, under a variety of pseudonyms.

'We going to carry him?'

'I think we're better off roping his ankles and dragging him.'

'Uh – Dad . . . look, I'll spell you.'

'What?'

'Carrying him. We can take turns.'

Without looking around, Jeff said, 'Right.' Jeff understood. Andy wasn't weak. Time was when he wouldn't have considered dragging a human being, either.

They took turns carrying the dead man with the ugly mouth and the big ugly burn across his body. He hadn't stepped on the wire apparently. He must've stumbled across something else and fallen on it. The first wire, probably, since Jeff had had to re-cover both of them.

There were two wires, forming concentric circles around this part of the hill, closing their circuits in the house. But the first one was just plain coated wire, without electricity. It hadn't been designed to trip a trespasser so that he fell on the second one, four feet inward. Jeff had put it there as a decoy, assuming that if someone found it he would treat it with great respect, stepping over it or maybe even cutting it while making certain he was well insulated. Then he would grin and certainly take his next several steps with confidence. Onto the second wire, hopefully. Or into one of the traps, set here and there within the second wire's perimeter.

The dead man was very heavy.

Jeff unshouldered him as they came to the last little bend in the gravel road. Around the short curve was the house. Without saying anything, he shoved the stiffish corpse into the luxuriant growth of blackberry and buckbushes and horse weeds–all floored with trickly laurel–beside the road.

'Let's just don't say anything about him.'

Andy nodded.

'I'll come out later and – get him. To fertilize the garden.'

Andy nodded. The shudder hardly showed.

He had seen bodies before. He had killed a man when he was thirteen, five years ago. He'd had to. And it had been just two years since he'd lost his sister. A marauding band of rippers from Off had grabbed her. From Lexington, most likely. Janie had been twelve. Pretty, slim, not even lumpy-chested yet.

Andy had heard the shots, six from his father's .30-30, and had snatched his own rifle and gone running. Age sixteen. Wearing a hip-strapped, leather-holstered pistol (if you can call dogskin leather) and carrying a rifle – which was not a boy's .22. When he arrived, having slowed and come silently, his father was just standing there, shaking. Around him lay five men, three of them naked, the others partially clothed and with their penises hanging out.

And Janie.

They were all dead. They had all raped her, and they'd done some other things, worse. Her eyes were open; she'd died conscious and in shock and horror and pain. Bleeding from cuts and scratches, bruised. And dead, with a smallish, blue-black hole just under her left nipple. She was naked.

Andy had nearly got himself shot; his father spun with wild eyes and Andy looked down the bore of that rifle and obeyed as if it were one more drill; he pumped one leg to hurl himself sideways, falling. But there'd been no shot. Jeff had recognized him and loosened his finger. His reflexes were as fast as they'd been back when he was sixteen – or if they had slowed, they must have been phenomenal then.

'The . . . animals we burn,' Jeff Andrews said. 'Janie we bury. Go back to the house, tell everyone else to sit tight except Alex and your mother. Tell them quietly we've found something, and bring shovels and the pick.'

Andy frowned. 'Mother—?'

'Yeah. She'll have to see. Otherwise she'll never believe.'

'What – what did they do to her?'

'They stuck things in her, and they all raped her,' Jeff said quietly. 'And cut her . . . parts, too, for fun, and her fingers are broken. All of them, I think.' He looked around at the bodies. 'See the black shirts? They're antifems. Go around killing women because it's women who have babies and population's the problem.' His jaw tightened until it looked ready to snap, like an overstretched wire. 'But they don't have anything against using their victims first.'

'Janie.'

Jeff looked at him. 'Yes.' Very quietly. 'Are you all right, son?'

'No, sir. I'm going to throw up, I think.'

'Right. After that, just – oh, god.'

He hadn't been able to keep it up. He wasn't a soldier or a general, never had been. He was a scholar, a writer, a man who'd spent most of his life with his fingers holding a book open or spidering over typewriter keys. Janie was twelve. He went straight down, folding a little and making a sick-dog noise, and Andy had a moment's horrible thought that his father was having a heart attack at forty-one. He wasn't. He just squat-knelt there, shaking, with his head down. Then he turned and sort of crawled a little and hugged the dead child and got blood all over his clothes.

Jeff went to the house.

When Jeff brought them back, Josie Andrews screamed and dropped to her knees to clutch her daughter's body to her, and she got blood on her clothes, too. They covered Janie with her father's clothing. And carried her up to the little hill just above the house, the one that they wished weren't there because it complicated defense, and Jeff and Andy and Alex dug a grave and they buried Janie there beside the garden, and two years later when Jeff and Andy found a dead man on the wire in the woods Andy helped carry him in, and he hardly shuddered at all when Jeff had said what he would do, later, without telling the others: cut the man up into several pieces and distribute them here and there, buried, to fertilize their soil.

The garden, after all, was a damsight more important than ancient superstitions and burial customs.

Chapter Two

The house was about sixty years old. Solid brick, built by a man who had owned the brick kiln at the foot of the hill. Solid brick, to the top of the ridgepole, and lined with firebrick. It stood atop a hill on three or four mostly wooded and mostly vertical acres.

First you turned off Federal Highway 60, onto State 174. A mile later you turned off again, on to an unnumbered county road called Bearskin, and off that a few seconds later onto the gravel road. The gravel road ran up and up at about a thirty-degree angle, then leveled off and shot up again, this time more steeply for a tenth of a mile, curving strongly at the summit. At the top was the chimney of the frame house that had stood there before the rip-off one night seven years ago. Jeff and Alex had buried them.

Past the chimney standing so lonely and dark above the weed-grown remains of what had been the Fraley Place, ran a dirt road that actually started back down the hill, paralleling the main road. (You could have crossed the little wooden bridge over the branch, but you didn't; it was a trap.) You came to an old frame house, sitting halfway up a wooded hillside. Its back was armor-plated. On a lower terrace was the garden. Arlie Eldridge lived there, with his second wife. She was twenty years younger than he, and she was from Off. With them lived his sons Red and Beadle, and their women. In all there were four children.

Past their house lay the ruins of two other houses. That part of the hill was Eldridge's, his to live on, farm, enjoy, and to defend. The barrel of the .30-caliber machine gun stared out at the dirt road from the new porch: concrete blocks, double thick.

A quarter-mile along the 'main' gravel road from Eldridge's and the Old Fraley Place there was another shell. This one wasn't weed-grown, and the shell had been reinforced. It stood on another upthrusting portion of the main hill. That house was a large frame, before it burned, naturally, one winter night. Too many old frame houses used to burn on cold winter nights hereabouts, in the western outskirts of Appalachia.

The road curved to pass where Jeff Andrews' garage used to be. He tore it down. It sat right beside the road, which was on a little terrace above the level of his house.

The garage was nice, but it was also a nice place for rippers to use as a fortress in an attack on the Andrews place. There had been several. A thick forsythia hedge used to run along the road above his house, too. Grieving at the loss of greenery and the pretty border of it, he'd torn it out. It had afforded cover for possible rippers.

The gutted frame on the knoll above the road just above Jeff's house belonged to Alex's father. After it burned, Alex's father left. Jeff and Alex bought the land, and they planted their garden where Alex's father used to plant his. Their dogs, long-eared mostly-beadles and a black-and-tan, were offsprings of Alex's father's too many dogs.

Below, on a semicircular terrace about a hundred yards wide by three hundred long, stood Jeff Andrews' house. Solid red brick, old, built to stay, built with money. It was bigger than when Jeff and Josie Andrews had bought it and turned it into what Jeff called the Writing Factory. Nine years ago he and Alex made their agreement. They pulled Alex's house apart, with some help from Red Eldridge and others – trading work, labor for labor, the way it used to be on adjacent farms – and added about half the brick onto Jeff's house. They used new wood.

They left Alex's basement where it was, except that they floored it, four feet in, with plywood. Very thin plywood. Rising above the trap thus formed, nearer Jeff's house, was a brick wall, most of the rest of the brick from Alex's house. Ten feet high, the wall stood just on the edge of that disguised basement.

Rippers had tried coming that way only once. They had seen the wall and immediately thought it would make a fine bulwark from behind which they could attack Jeff's place, once they crossed the old flooring to get to it. And of course the flooring gave way, and the light started flashing in Jeff's house and the alarm went off. And Jeff and Alex had to run out with their guns, and they found that they had trapped four rippers, two with broken legs, one with a broken neck and the fourth a sprained wrist and a genuine Thompson submachine gun. He just missed Alex. Later Jeff and Alex had to go into town to buy some plywood and reset the trap – incidentally roofing a mausoleum in which rested four men.

On Jeff's side of the brick wall were four sets of steps,

making the wall a masterpiece of medieval defensive construction, complete with disguised moat.

The four-foot wall around Jeff's front porch he and Alex had raised from two feet nine years ago.

The windows were equipped with city-type push-button screens, iron. The house contained nearly enough assorted artillery to supply a Guard unit, although without so much ammunition. There was plenty, though, including belts for the two machine guns and clips for the Thompson.

Alex's son Roger was the youngest member of the Jeff-Alex household. He was ten, and a crack shot. He could even operate the machine gun mounted in the attic window; it swept the knoll-top garden. Jeff's blonde daughter Kristy was fifteen. She carried a holstered gun, a .32 revolver just like her mother's. She could use it. She also knew how to use the knife she wore on a sort of garter-belt arrangement holding it on her left thigh; Kristy was left-handed.

The house stood on the edge of a hillside, a sheer drop of over a hundred feet at an angle of something like sixty or maybe seventy degrees. Below ran the big road. State 174. If you didn't turn off it onto the unnumbered county road at the foot of the hill's south side, you continued on 174 and passed the house, a couple of hundred yards below, on the northwest.

From the second floor, the Jeff-Alex household could see all the way up the big road to the old railroad crossing at the highway: U.S. 60, a mile away.

'The U.S.,' Jacob Hay wrote in a magazine article in 1968, 'is still a country of great uninhabited stretches of land where entirely new metropolitan centers can be designed to satisfy the needs and, indeed, delight the tastes of the residents.'

Uh-huh, some people thought, and we're going to double the population by the turn of the century, and we're at 200 million now and the ideal population for America is about three-quarters that.

By 1978, people were predicting at the same time Mr.

Hay was writing his article, 70 percent of the country's population will live in the cities.

Uh-huh, Jeff Andrews thought, but not me!

As it turned out the prediction was off a little. The figure was more than 70 percent, using a loose definition of "city" so that you included any collection of houses with a post office and some stores. There weren't so many of those anymore. Towns creepered out to envise them; cities flowed out to grasp the towns.

At about the same time, his city becoming an open wound festering on the edge of water it had so filthied as to be incapable of cleaning the wound, Mayor Yorty of Los Angeles announced his solution to the Vietnamese war. Few listened to the solution of a man whose city was spurting up pus about his ankles.

In that same year the Mayor of New York City – not an open wound, but a gangrenous one – strongly criticized the President's State or the Union message. (The President was not in the Mayor's political party.) The essence of his criticism was that the President of all these states had not promised enough largesse for the mayor's city. Thus he admitted his own inability to do that which he was paid to do: govern, manage, enforce, solve problems. It was hard to blame him too strongly: the problems were already past solution.

Andy and Kristy and Scott and Roger had studied those things last week. This afternoon the lesson continued, in the living room, gathered around Jeff. He held sway in his old chair, thrice-recovered, this last time in red terry over the naugahyde that roasted his butt and gave him a sweat-sore crack.

'Scott,' he said, and his younger son nodded.

'The Federal Police Force was created to aid the consistently louder-screaming mayors in fighting the riptide of crime. They—'

'Shit, son, that's straight out of the book. *Tell* me.'

'The . . . the cities,' Scott said, frowning, 'were, ah, boiling with crime. The police couldn't handle it. Every time it got really bad, more than just the normal everyday murders and robberies and stuff, the National Guard or the militia, sometimes the State Police, would come in.'

'And almost always in college demonstrations,' Alex's son Roger said. 'The FPF *also* saved the government from the revolution that would've happened, probably in the seventies. It was Washington saving itself.' Poll parrot; he'd heard Jeff say that. Jeff went after causes, root causes.

Jeff nodded without taking his eyes off Scott. He hadn't called on Roger.

'So Washington – the Congress – created the Federal Police Force. The war on crime became a war.'

Jeff nodded. 'OK. Who won?'

Silence, then Kristy said, 'Nobody. The war's still on.'

'True. Who's winning?'

'They are.'

'Who's they, Kristy?'

'The . . . criminals.'

'And who are the criminals?' Jeff Andrews went after the answers under the answers. Aristole and Rand had taught him to move back through one effect after another until he came to the Cause. He was looking at Andy.

They looked at him. Andy scratched his chest. Scott grinned.

'Scott?' He hated to call on Scott all the time; the quiet boy was so *bright*.

'There aren't any,' Scott said. 'Everybody. Break a law and you're a criminal, right then. But it might be you tried to steal because you were hungry, and you killed because you were about to get caught. I mean, you always have criminals, "criminal types." But when things get the way they are now, you have a lot more.'

'Why?'

'Population,' Roger said.

'Population. And what do we do about that?'

'Well . . . you don't have four kids like you and Mom did,' Scott said.

Jeff smiled, nodding. 'True. True. It was a religious thing, as we've told you. We outgrew it, but we'd already had four kids. Mea culpa.'

'Should've stopped at two,' Scott said, giving Kristy a *girls!* look.

'Or one,' Andy said, grinning at his brother.

Kristy said nothing, and suddenly there was silence. Yes. They should have stopped at three, and then there'd have been no Janie, and no grave up on the hill at the edge of the garden.

Of the kids, only Andy knew about that grave, and he wasn't sure he knew. That is, about Janie. He had heard six shots from his father's rifle. Five dead men. Each with one hole in him. And a dead Janie. With one hole in her. Had his father missed with that sixth shot, or – was he really that strong, really that brave? Because that's what it would have taken, and Andy knew damned well he didn't have that kind of strength and bravery and guts. Had it been up to him it would all have been worse; Janie would still be here with them. But – not really. Because she'd be someone else, both in her mind and in her body. Teeth broken, fingers broken, nose smashed, body cut. . . .

He wasn't sure, of course. All five of her attackers had been armed. Maybe one of them had shot her; probably. He had wondered about it, many times. He had found himself hoping, lately, that she had been alive and that Dad had shot her. Because that would have been the right thing to do, and it made the man more than strong, almost a god. And that's what it took, to survive.

'In the great stretches of glass and concrete and steel that hide the natural landscape,' Jane Whitbread had written, 'where is there one long view of earth and sky to show the seasons or rest the eye, or a silent place to rest the car? Or the space to stretch and play, or to be still and alone?'

Here. On the hill. It was almost The Hill. Like a fortress, a fortified keep, a castle standing high above the road and the squirming, rotting, festering world. At least that's the way Andy Andrews thought of it.

'What did the cities do?' Jeff Andrews asked, to break the silence. The question was a ritual, and so was the answer:

'They shouted HELP, HELP, Big Brother!' – Roger.

'And what happens when you shout help help Big Brother?' – Jeff.

'CAIN COMES!' – chorus. Chuckles.

'Daddy?'

Jeff looked at Kristy. Cute girl, he thought, better looking than I am, probably prettier than her mother. Blonde hair like month-old straw, a lot of it, presently pulled back carelessly and tied with something bright blue, even darker than her eyes. Super bright – and with about as much common sense as the wood tick her mother had removed from that pretty hair yesterday.

His eyebrows-up look acknowledged and invited her question.

'Dad – who will I marry?'

Oh god, Kristy honey, who will you marry? I've thought about that and thought about it. Somebody from Town, because we have to do it? Somebody who'll either take you there to live in that mixed metaphor of a slimehole/sardine can? Or Roger, maybe, by default, because he's here? Why did you have to ask that one, baby?

He smiled and shrugged. 'How do I know, babe? Maybe Roger.'

'Bluh!'

'Ye-e-e-ech!' Roger agreed.

'So much for that,' Jeff grinned, but there was a lost look in his eyes, a question behind them. *Dad? Who will I marry?*

Education by television and by daddy. Contact with other students: zero.

Social contacts: zero.

Possibilities: well, if not zero, close on. Close on.

The world was going to hell on an overcrowded pogo stick and the only way to 'govern' such a world was tightly. With the Federal Police Force, with heavy taxes to support it and aid to keep the cities alive, with heavy social security to provide for those who might make it to age 55 and mandatory retirement, with no public gatherings – including schools.

And here and there there were little pockets, castle keeps, shielded and guarded. Here and there were men like Jeff Andrews, raising his own family and educating it too, raising his own food and associating with the outside world – which began at the foot of the hill – as little as possible. More than surviving: living. Accepting nothing. Self-sufficient. And shielded. Shielding his children and his wife from the horrors of the cities, from the horrors of the towns, of the townships and hamlets, of the roads between them. And feeding them, feeding them well and regularly. Meat when it was available in town; Hoodie gave him a phone call, usually. Otherwise squirrel, rabbit, possum; even mole and mice, now and then. Chickens traded with Arlie Eldridge. Vegetables from the garden. And the concentrated stuff that formed the sole food of so many throughout the country, along with soybeans: spacefood.

The country was surviving on spacefood, concentrates designed for astronauts, and the country was losing its teeth.

But – who was Kristy going to marry? And Scott? And Andy, Andy the oldest, the kid who was at the peak of his sexual powers, supposedly, and was certainly handjobbing himself with great regularity.

He'll have to go out and get himself a girl, Jeff thought, and in his mind he saw a sort of Gustave Dore scene of the Romans, grabbing the Sabine women so that one day hundreds of years later Poppaea Sabina could be Nero's mistress, then wife.

And then another thought, uglier. *Somewhere, right now,* Jeff realized, *someone else is thinking the same thing I am, about his son. He'll have to go to get himself a woman. And . . . here's Kristy.*

Not while I live!

Which, of course, that other father was also thinking, which meant that Andy might well set off in search of a bride and never come home.

We'll all go, Jeff thought. *A wifenapping expedition for Andy!*

And he told himself; *Ridiculous!*

'Maybe we could all go to Sweden,' Andy said, 'and find us some brides and grooms.'

This morning, Jeff thought, *it was Australia; this afternoon it's Sweden. He dreams, he's restless, and what am I doing about it? What can I do about it? I ought to go out and kidnap a girl! From a city – she'd be glad enough to be here, once she breathed a little air and saw some white clouds and found she could go outside and walk around, barefoot on real grass, without danger. I'll bet I could work out something, in town. Who has a daughter about Andy's age – with a brain?* He stared at the ceiling, thinking.

'Sweden isn't taking any people,' Kristy said. 'Don't you ever watch the news? They turned away an airliner seven British had hijacked, just yesterday. Wouldn't even let it land.'

'What,' Roger asked, 'is so good about Sweden?'

'It's the fastest growing democracy in the world,' Kristy said.

'The fastest growing capitalism, you mean,' Scott said.

She tried to wither him with a down-the-nose stare. 'What's the difference, dummy?'

'It's coming on like Japan, forty years ago,' Andy said quietly. 'They're happy over there.'

Kristy faced around to Roger. 'Socialism practically destroyed Sweden in the eighties, and now it's growing faster than anyplace. It's lessy-fair.'

'It's what?'

Jeff grinned. 'Lassay-fair,' he said. He spelled it out: *laissez faire*. 'A free society based on tit for tat.'

'That's just what we've got here,' Andy said, jerking erect and proclaiming it proudly in a red-white-and-blue tone of voice.

'Good grass,' Scott sneered, 'this country's been giving tit without regard for tat ever since about 1930! Dad, he just isn't reading or thinking either.'

'I read all the time.'

'Fiction!'

'COOL IT!'

They looked chastened before Jeff's shout and his gaze, and both boys' lips moved: *Sorry, sir.*

'Anyhow,' Andy said, 'Sweden's about the greatest place in the world, right now.'

'Well I think—'

'Excuse me, Kristy, but I want to ask Andy something about that,' Jeff said. 'Andy – you said a minute ago that they're happy over there. As if that's the only place in the world where anybody's happy.'

Andy looked at him. 'Close on.'

'You're not happy, then.'

Andy twisted his face, gave his father a look. 'Out of bounds, Dad. That's intimidation.'

'*Lord, I'm happy*!' Kristy advised the world.

'Me too!' Scott looked at his brother. 'Do they have cities over there?'

'Of course.'

Scott shrugged. 'Well then. Some people in Sweden are happy, just like some are here. People like us. You can't be happy and live in a city, too.'

'I'd sure hate to live in a city!'

'I wouldn't even want to visit one!'

Jeff sat back, looking at them, through them. Had he gone too far? Had he done this to them, or was it the fault of – whom? The government? The cowardice of some about things like abortion legislation and family-planning from HEW, which was needed at least twenty-five years before it began? The religious bigotry of others, who screamed that a fetus was a life and its termination was murder, that it should be protected and cherished and given civil rights – without offering any solution for the continuation of those protections and rights once it became a cerebrating human being? The use of ecology as a political tool, rather than a skull and bones staring the country in the face? Maybe he was just an oddball. He had bought this place and lived out here, eight miles from Morehead, even before it became *necessary* that he live here, and fortify first his home, then his property, then the (his) hill.

'Twenty minutes till Calvin Blue, Dad,' Andy told him.

Jeff glanced at his watch. Why, he told himself angrily, do I do that, as if I'm checking on him?

'Andy's right. Calvin Blue and the News in twenty minutes, folks. Hoes all around for fifteen minutes in the garden. Let's go.'

MEANWHILE: I

A City Is A Terrible Place to Visit, but I'd Sure Hate To Live There

Leonard Rosebury watched in shock as the big car passed him easily on the left. Everyone was watching, he noticed. Or appeared to be, by the position of their heads. It was hard to tell where people were looking when everyone wore one-way glasses, but you learned to gauge by the way their heads were turned, even by their eyebrows, when they weren't wearing the goggle-type affairs that covered brows and most of the nose too.

It was an ancient automobile, a gasoline-engine dinosaur, right here in the city! Noisy, roaring and growling (although he couldn't hear it) capable of speeds like up to a hundred miles an hour or so, maybe more. A road car. A country car, moving unconcernedly along among the almost silent miniks and maxis. As if the driver owned the damned street, as if he had a right to put out all that poison!

Leonard Rosebury checked the pollution gauge on the instrument panel before him. He was amazed that its needle did not jump all the way across the gauge. It moved constantly, of course, but he was sure the needle's little quiver up the scale was caused by the monster.

The son of a bitch!

Why didn't he drive on, get away from here, stop trying to kill poor Leonard Rosebury in his electric minik, all the other Leonard Roseburys in *their* towncars, all the people crowded together in the big double-decker electric maxibuses? Certainly he had the power. The son of a bitch! Where the hell were the police?

The minik in front of Leonard swung off the freeway, angling down the ramp onto the approach to Market and the West End. The minik in front of that one swung into the center lane, and Leonard increased his speed almost to maximum. Racing along at thirty miles per hour, he watched the back end of the maxi ahead rush toward him.

Then he had to jam on his brakes, cursing, his eyes bulging, as the gasoline dinosaur whipped into his lane, directly in front of him. God, the speed and pickup of that thing! But – how the devil was the driver able to handle it? It was so huge. Five or six passengers, Leonard remembered, and right up to a hundred miles an hour, on the Interstates. His father had had one, Leonard had even ridden in it, but he couldn't remember, not really. His father had moved into St. Louis when Leonard was seven, looking for better work than the farm dominated by unpredictable weather, for better housing than the ramshackle farmhouse, for better living conditions than direct exposure to countless insects and ever-changing weather and all the other horrors of farm life.

Leonard shivered, glancing about for a way to get out from behind the old automobile. He couldn't. Before him, behind him, on either side of him were solid lines of miniks and maxis, moving thousands and thousands of persons home from work, to work from home, to this place or that. Mingled among them were the blue and white of city police vehicles, armed and armored, and the shivery brown and green vehicles, tanklike affairs with windshields that could be closed just like a house's window. Feps. And here was he, Leonard Rosebury, sixteen thousand a year and in the fifty-three percent tax bracket and damned proud of it – stuck behind a poison-breathing dragon from the past!

It was from out of town, of course. Such monsters were illegal in cities. They were poison. He knew his ecohistory. Sometime in the sixties – he wasn't sure of the year – fourteen thousand tons of guck had been added to the air above Los Angeles every day. It wasn't enough that the city was a cesspool, but even its air had become a garbage dump. And over 87 percent of that guck came from just such a monster as the one bellowing along so unconcernedly right in front of Leonard Rosebury, right here in the *city*!

One of Leonard's childhood memories was the arrival of the Rosebury family in St. Louis. How strange that dark sky had looked, how he had stared and wondered at it. (You don't study "photochemical smog" in the first grade.)

'Daddy,' he asked, 'what's that? Why's the air so dark?'

'That's civilization, son,' his father told him, not without pride. 'That comes from the factories where Daddy's going to work and make good money and have a nice house with neighbors and ice-cream men and everything.'

'That's what killed the crops,' Mom said.

But it hadn't been factories. The factories were doing their part, of course, in poisoning the air, but their speciality was rivers. The broad, broad old river they crossed to get into the city and crossed, and crossed. It had been the automobiles, cars just like the one they were riding in, but they hadn't known it then. And then out of the midday darkness had loomed the enormous metal arch, its feet vanishing into the closely crowded buildings, its arching summit vanishing into the darkness above. And little Lennie Rosebury had forgotten all about darkness at noon, and the thought didn't occur to him in those terms until he was twenty years old and had to read Arthur Koestler.

Helplessly following the old automobile, a relic from the days of the triumphant domination of the country by what Lewis Mumford had called Detroit's infantile fantasies, Leonard tried to remember. Let's see, that thing was spewing out lead, and who hadn't heard of lead poisoning? And an assortment of organic compounds and nitrogen oxides, which were the prime sources – with sunlit oxygen – in the smog of the old days. Then there was carbon monoxide, and everybody knew that was poison, and if you got to the point where you really couldn't take it anymore you could always go into the garage and let your automobile carry you off to eternity, without even moving.

Let's see, was that all – oh god no! There were sulfur oxides, too; they were really nice, here on the river. They combined with water vapor to form a lovely compound known fancily at H_2SO_4. Sulfuric acid. What that did to nylon stockings and the like was nothing compared to what it had done to Leonard Rosebury's mother.

He began to sweat.

The car ahead did have an afterburner. But after all – what had that ever solved? There had been one on the next car his father bought, seven years after his arrival here in the land of milk and honey. (That was the year they were able to move out of East St. Louis. Luckily; the next year it was proclaimed sovereign and separatist, a part of the Black Nation of Aframerika.) His father had been very proud of that new car with its afterburner. It eliminated the stuff everyone could pronounce, by then: the horrible hydrocarbons, worst menace since Communism. But, born in California like so many other pernicious horrors with attractive exterior wrappings, the afterburners didn't last long.

Since the car ahead of Leonard Rosebury had an afterburner, it wasn't filling the air with hydrocarbons, which killed slowly, building and building toward doomsday. No. It was now squirting out pound after pound of nitrogen oxides. They had always reacted with the hydrocarbons, and now they were liberated, and it didn't take long to learn that they were worse. (Or better; it was a matter of personal preference. Would you rather die quickly or slowly?) Not as patient as the hydrocarbons, the nitroxides killed swiftly, attacking several places at once. Leonard could well remember his constantly bleeding nose, and the thousands and millions of other almost permanently sore noses, as mucous membranes reacted in helpless agony to the nitroxides emitted by their after-burner-safe automobiles.

Sweating, biting his lower lip, he tried frantically to get into the left lane. Nothing doing. He saw the other driver's mouth moving in (deserved) vituperation before he opaqued the window on that side of the car.

Leonard was two miles from his exit. Why wasn't someone *doing* something? Tentatively he raised a finger to his nose, pushed carefully. He looked at the finger. No blood. He tried holding his breath, wishing he'd had his minik's oxyrator checked last Saturday. Maybe he was safe, so long as he remained in his minik with the oxyrator on. He reached over to switch it on full, listening to its whine with a little frown. Why were the local police and the Feps letting that guy just drive along here this way, right in town, killing them all?

He glanced around. Where had they gone? There wasn't a police vehicle in sight. Funny, there had been several, just a minute ago. He must have been thinking about something else and failed to notice when they gunned off. Probably over to West Side again. So somebody was getting ripped, or some damned girl was getting herself raped, or somebody had got pissed off and was sniping or torching a building or two. Serve them right, the scum. So what the hell, this creature up ahead was poisoning *thousands*. He was complacently killing *Leonard Rosebury*, him and his stinking iron dinosaur with its Illinois plates!

Might know he wouldn't even be a Missourian!

Somebody did something. The electric towncars were not long on speed and pickup, but they were supremely parkable and maneuverable. Which was all they needed; what need of multi-horsepower in cities, when every vehicle was jammed together and couldn't get anywhere anyhow? But the man in front of and to the left of the gasoline monster swung his eminently maneuverable minik over in front of the automobile, and the Illinois driver responded with the usual reaction time, twenty or more seconds to get his foot from accelerator to brake, and Leonard jerked his foot off the accelerator as he realized the machine ahead had jolted to a stop. Instantly his minik responded to the decreased pressure on the pedal. Instantly it braked, and Leonard gasped and put a hand over pounding heart as he came to a stop a few feet from the back of the monster. He could read the strip of old, broken chrome, now: PONT AC.

He sat shaking in delayed reaction. The door of the old car swung open. A man swung out, a big man whose clothes didn't look right; they looked like *clothes*, perm stuff, rather than the city-dweller's usual uniform of disposables. He saw the man's broad shoulders and small butt move forward, around his machine to the one that had pulled in front of him. Then Leonard saw the other driver, also out on the pavement. Lord, he was a garink, his suit showed that clearly; it was one of the disposables the government handed out once monthly to everyone on the guaranteed income rolls. The guy was a $7500-a-year man, for god's sake!

Leonard cut off his engine. Well, he had status, his own paid-for jacsuit would show that. He'd go stick up for the guy, a fellow St. Louisan, and while he was at it he'd raise hell with that out-of-state hick in his poison-breathing monstrosity of an illegal vehicle! Using left thumb and right hand to unlock the door, he pushed it open.

And yanked it shut, wincing: the noise! He'd forgotten, sealed up in the fortress keep of his car and in his frightened fury. Quickly he stuffed in his earplugs, deciding against the respirator. He got out of the car. Already others were stopping, too. Getting out.

'—right out in front of me that way!' the auto driver was saying loudly, and even his accent was wrong.

'I gotta be in this lane, dammit! I turn off in two blocks. If you'd been driving a decent car you'd have stopped automatically. Now just look what you did to my minik!'

'I wish my foot'd slipped off the brake and ground you up into mincemeat, you damned smartass! Drive that car like some kind of a kid, no regard for anyone else whatever!'

'I really think,' Leonard Rosebury said, stepping up to them in his black-and-silver vylon suit, 'that you shouldn't be talking about regard for others.'

Both men looked at him. So did two or three others who'd got out to see what was the matter – and to give the out-of-stater a good piece of their minds. They were all silent for a moment as a jet bellowed over.

Leonard pointed disdainfully at the Pontiac. 'You come into the city in that thing, just driving along, poisoning us all and our kids—'

'Yeah,' a fat man in a shapeless charbrown jacsuit said,

'our kids!' He glanced around at the five or six others who'd stopped their cars to join him. 'Our kids! Lookit that thing he's driving! A regular old poison factory. Don't you know the law about city cars, buddy?'

The big man from Illinois looked around, frowning. 'I was just—'

'—scaring the life out of all of us,' Leonard said, 'not to *mention* polluting our air and endangering the lives of our kids.'

There was a dissonant chorus of agreement from the eight or ten others gathered about. The Illinoiser looked around at the faces, eyeless because of the opaque glasses.

'Look, I'm on my way home, I had to come in to get a part for this thing,' the out-of-stater said. 'I'm not crazy about it myself – it's all I can afford. I didn't have the *money* to rent a minik at the edge of town.'

'Shit,' the man he'd hit snapped. 'All you had to do was show'em your card, Jack. You wouldna had to pay.'

The big man seemed to grow taller. 'Card!' He spat the words out. 'I don't have any card – I raise food, mister, and sell it to feed you city people so you don't starve. I made over four thousand last year, but I be damned if I'll accept anything from the government! That ain't right!'

God, Leonard thought, doesn't the mongoloid idiot KNOW he's talking with a garink? There were several others, too, in the twelve or thirteen men gathered around the scene of the accident.

Silence. Wide-eyed, staring silence. Naturally: how long had it been since they'd heard anything like that, since anyone had *dared* indicate there was something wrong with accepting enough money from the Federal Government to bring your income up to a livable seventy-five hundred?

'Well you – you better have *insurance*!' the fat man said.

'IT WASN'T MY FAULT! HE PULLED RIGHT IN FRONT OF ME! I COULDN'T—'

'Hasn't got INSURANCE!'

'Poisoning our KIDS!'

'Everybody in St. Louis may be sick tomorrow, just because of this son of a bitch – and he isn't even from MISSOURI!'

CRASH.

No one knew who threw the brick, or where he'd found it. (Probably carried it in his car; sensible!) No one ever knew who started things. It just came flying through the air, whizzed past the out-of-stater's face, and smashed into the door of his old pale-blue Pontiac.

He bellowed, stared at the ugly dent, and turned horrified, enraged eyes on the clot of angry St. Louisans. Then he bent for the brick.

'Watch out!' the fat man yelled. 'He's gonna throw that brick at us!'

CRASH.

Another brick; this one slammed into the Pontiac's window, right at the doorsill, and dropped onto the driver's back. He grunted. The window starred. The brick rolled off. With the first brick in his right hand, he reached for the second.

The fat man stepped forward and jammed his booted foot down on the sun-browned hand.

The man behind him bent quickly and snatched up the brick.

The Illinoiser hit the fat man's calf and ankle with the brick in his right hand. The fat man screamed. The man beside him swung up his brick and threw it and a rock came arching in from behind him, from an invisible hand again, and the driver of the minik hit by the Pontiac snarled and bent to pick up the rock after it bounced off the Illinoiser's upper arm, and Leonard felt a surge of anger and desire to punish this man who had endangered their lives and insulted them all and the Illinoiser vanished beneath a wave of cursing, stamping, pummeling St. Louisans. Some used fists, others feet, others briefcases or whatever they had in their cars for defense: macesticks and wrenches and the like.

Leonard Rosebury took a wrench across the wristwatch and staggered back, his hand dangling. He moaned. The fat man fell out of the mass of twisting, swinging, writhing bodies with blood all over his face. Someone screamed. The Illinoiser seemed to make no noise at all, just flailing and grabbing and taking blow after blow.

'Put 'im back in his sinking car and get the sonuvabitch off OUR freeway!' someone yelled.

They put him back in his sinking car, limp and bleeding and helpless, and they slammed the door. Then they put their backs to it and got the sonuvabitch off their freeway.

By the time the FPF chopper – a terrible polluter, but what are you going to do? – swung down overhead, twenty or thirty men were straining, and the old Pontiac was poised, both left tires off the ground by a foot or more.

'STOP WHAT YOU'RE DOING AND MOVE ON AT ONCE!' the big voice bellowed down from the Fep chopper.

One last good strain and the old Pontiac and its driver went off the freeway. It dropped ten feet, struck a support with a terrible clang and shrieking grate of metal on metal, catapulting it outward. It dropped another thirty feet and sheared off a flagpole just before smashing at an angle across the top front of Borstelmann's Delly. The top and front of Borstelmann's Delly resisted momentarily, then went on down onto the sidewalk and street with the Pontiac. Mrs. Martin A. Cowen and her daughter Jean were killed instantly. Miraculously, little Stevie, whizzing down the sidewalk in the pram his mother had been pushing, was totally unhurt. Ike Borstelmann rushed out of his store, looked upward at the faces staring down at him from the freeway, and ran back into his delly.

'EMERGENCY IS DECLARED,' the Fep man overhead warned with his microphone, and the man whose minik had been hit in the rear by the Illinoiser jumped into his machine and drove off as fast as he could. The chopper rocked in air as a jet went over.

'LAST WARNING,' the Feps in the chopper said.

Bleeding profusely from the face, the fat man got to one knee and then to his feet and started lurching toward his car.

'Here this one's getting away,' a man shouted. He had just pulled up and stopped, and he reached back into his car and grabbed a defenser and swung it. The needly little beam of light cut the fat man half in two, cauterizing the wound nicely.

Leonard Rosebury, moaning and clutching his broken wrist close to his chest, tried to push his way to his car.

'Where the shit you think you're going, buddy,' a man snarled, and Leonard had an instant's view of a garink suit-sleeve before the fist emerging from it slammed into his left eye.

'Lookit the suit the bastard's wearing,' the man said, kicking Leonard as he collapsed. 'Rich son of a bitch!'

Below, Ike Borstelmann emerged from his delly and, almost without aiming, let go with both barrels of his old shotgun.

Seven or eight men screamed as pellets struck their faces and necks and hands, and other pellets tink-tinked off the hovering chopper.

The door-mounted laser sent a light-pencil down to widow Mrs. Ike Borstelmann. The man behind the gunner tossed three gas grenades out to burst on the freeway. Stupid, but even Feps make mistakes. Extraordinary powers aren't conducive to making a man stop and think carefully. The sound was drowned by the screaming whoosh of a jet in takeoff.

Six men jumped from the freeway to their deaths, in an attempt to escape the vomit-gas. Three others fell or were knocked over. Within seven minutes thirty-one miniks and three buses were piled up in the swirling mist of yellow-pink gas.

They dragged Leonard Rosebury from under one of the maxis three hours later, but by that time he had bled to death. Besides, everyone was very very busy with the riot in the street below. The torched automobile and ensuing riot eventually burned out three-point-two blocks, or so the official reports said.

Mrs. Rosebury waited supper till ten-thirty. Then came the phone call from Fep, and she fainted.

Chapter Three

'D'you think we should eat them?'

Jeff nodded. 'Yes. I think we'd better. I think we have to.'

Josie frowned up at him. 'Well . . . not all the peas are red, Jeff.'

'Yeah. But next year they probably will be. It's pollution, mutation. How do we know from what? You and I are both carrying enough Azodrin in our bodies, chlorinated hydrocarbons, to commit large-scale insecticide right now. How long since you've seen a really blue sky, a really clean white cloud, babe? And we're way the hell away from any industry, except a couple of lumberyards that are mostly closed because of the Reforestation Laws.' He sighed, rolling the two young peas in his palm. They were quite red. The opened pod was red-tinged, though still green. They'd outlawed DDT long ago. So the petroleum companies had brought out new substitutes.

'You don't think they're poison, sweetheart?'

'I do indeed think they're poison, Josiebabe. About everything we eat is poison, and the air we breathe, too. The well is closed, and we don't know how deep it is, but surely even our water isn't pure hydrogen-oxygen compound. We've been eating and drinking and breathing poison for a half-century or more, honey, of all kinds. The alternative is to stop breathing and eating and drinking and that just ain't satisfactory.'

She stood up, glanced frowning down at the rows of convoluting pea-plants, and back at his face. She slid her hands absently down her blue-jeaned hips. They were a pretty damned good set of hips, he thought, and he'd told her so enough times so that even she believed it. All women couldn't be built like Ellen Fonda, which to Jeff Andrews was very good news indeed. He preferred women to look like women, and Josie looked a lot more like a woman than many women.

'You think we're all dying slowly.'

He shook his head. 'No honey, I really don't. As a culture, even as a race, maybe. But not as individuals, no. We seem to be – evolving, or whatever the term is. Like the flies that developed an immunity to DDT, even before it was banned. Despite all the radiation and the warnings, we still aren't producing two-headed babies or kids with scales or whatever. The kids look just like us – except they have bigger *feet*, generation after generation. *Homo pachydermis,* that's us.' He smiled.

His wife did not return the smile. She waited.

'I think we are absorbing the changes,' he said quietly, forced to seriousness. 'Thriving on pollution. Grooving on bad air. We may even need it. Time may come when people will find some pure water somewhere, and drink some, and keel over dead or come down with some new disease. Or vomit at the sight of green peas, instead of red.' He flipped one of the firm little marbles into the air, squinted, missed catching it. He didn't look down.

'God,' she said, shaking her head.

'He may be interested,' Jeff said. 'Then again he may not. Maybe it's all part of a plan, for those who like to think there's a plan. You know, the theory you developed. That the campaign to save the bald iggle and the alligator may have been a mistake, that they were intended to go, as a part of things. The same way triceratops went, and the dodo, and later the American bison, and then pheasants, and elephants, and so on. All a part of things. This species and that has been dying, vanishing since the year One.'

Josie toed the nearest pea-plant – so rampantly twisting and full, now, that individual plants could scarcely be differentiated. She bent to pull a weed. When it came up with a nearly complete root system, she broke it carefully, so that the next rain mightn't set it growing again. She dropped it. Then she looked up at him again. The blue sunglasses turned the tinted contacts on her green eyes a deep turquoise.

'You think we're next?'

'I think as little as possible,' he said, palming her breast through the shirt she wore tied beneath her bosom.

'Don't give me that, Jeff. I'm serious.'

'Sorry. I don't know, Josiebabe. I don't know. Seems to me that *if* we survive, we'll just be something else. Certainly we won't be the same sort of fellow Julius Caesar was. He lived with pollution, too, you know. The Tiber was full of shit most of the time and the Senators' glass factories got to be pretty bad places to work. But – there wasn't much of it. Skies were still blue. Fish still flowed with the streams. There were still salmon, then. Later, Napoleon littered the world with bodies and cannon smoke, and so did Lincoln-Davis-Lee-Grant.' He shrugged. 'Then things really started to change. And here we are, not conscious of any changes. Or not many. An awful lot of cancer. An awful lot of men going bald too soon. Women are increasingly titless or nearly, it seems to me. But I am *essentially* the same sort of crittur that Lincoln and Collidge were, and Andy's *essentially* the same as I am.'

'What about his children?' Josie's voice was almost a whisper.

Jeff shook his head. 'We were worried about ours, honey. They look swell, and they're a *bright* bunch of atomic-age mutants.'

'Kristy has that big birthmark on her back—'

'My grandmother had an almost identical one on her ass.'

She punched him in the belly. He pinched her breast, spun her about and slapped her fanny, then said, 'Watch you don't step on the food there, woman.'

She looked at him, smiling. 'You think we're going to make it.'

'Even on red peas,' he said. 'Man abides.'

Suddenly she chuckled, and when he fixed her with a questioning look, she said, 'Would you believe the Jolly Red Giant?'

That day he and Alex checked all the traps. They didn't bother checking them daily, although the circuit of the wire was made on a daily basis, in the morning just after breakfast. The traps were undisturbed.

They checked the two foxholes; they were fine. The drainage pipe from the road was going to *have* to be replaced. They went down-basement, crawled under the clothes-sorting table, and opened the little door into the wall. Inside was a sort of room, about three by four feet. It connected by a shaft to the floor of the fireplace in the living room above. The shaft and little "room", of course, had been built into the house by a man who preferred merely dropping fireplace ashes into the basement and making a grand now-and-then task of carting out the ashes, rather than bucketing them daily out of the fireplace itself.

Now there was another door, and they opened it and crawled along the tunnel they had dug three years ago. It was damp, it was musty-smelling, and they wrinkled their noses and blinked and twitched their heads as they pushed them through spider webs.

'Spiders really 'preciate this tunnel,' Alex said, his voice hollow behind Jeff.

'Yeah. At least a bunch of snakes haven't set up housekeeping in here. Think I'll start boning up on mushrooms. Might as well use this nice dark hole.'

He came to the tunnel's end, put out his light – the miner's hat came in handy, and who needed miner's hats anymore? John L. Lewis had begun the destruction of the coal industry, by getting his workers such excellent money that the mineowners couldn't afford people anymore. They put in more and more machinery. And took to strip-mining, which managed to remain legal just long enough to destroy nearly as much of the Eastern Kuntucky hills as American bombs had destroyed the countryside of Vietnam. The important Appalachian industry had managed to hang on for a while, once someone learned how to use coal in making asphalt – and the war between the concreters and the asphalters began. Both had been used in Interstates, even in Kentucky and Pennsylvania and West Virginia. Had we been as chauvinistic and xenophobic then as now, Jeff mused, all roads in those coal states would have been asphalt, surely.

At any rate, the miners' hats with their little lights were of some value now, and Jeff and Alex had acquired an even dozen of them.

After switching off his hardhat light, Jeff squinted carefully at the back wall of the tunnel, striving to find a hint of light. There was none. Excellent.

'OK,' he said, and waited. Alex started backing out, and after he was sure his feet wouldn't meet Alex's face, Jeff, too, crawdaddied out of the tunnel.

They went back upstairs and out of the house and over the hill.

On the side of the house that stood above the big road, they stood for a moment to gaze down at it.

No one dragged off down there every Saturday night anymore. They didn't hear the sound of guitars and fiddles and twanging Bluegrass voices down there on Saturdays and Sundays anymore. They seldom saw cars, either, and then only electric town cars. Trucks, now and then. And occasionally the green and brown trucks of the FPF.

They went over the hill.

Five feet down, the basement pipe, the house's main drainage system, emerged to empty into the cesspool several feet below. Just beside that, dangerously close, the basement tunnel emerged into a tangled thicket of horseweeds and pokeberry, all crowding around the wild peach trees. The trees and weeds grew tall and strong and profuse there, thriving on the earth around the cesspool. They had planted and nurtured forsythia down here, and it too grew wildly and rampantly. The bases of some stalks were an inch in diameter, and when the tangled bushes bloomed it was in an explosion of bright yellow flowers.

All of it covered the mouth of the tunnel from the basement very effectively. It was a tunnel they inspected frequently, but never wanted to use. It was an escape hatch.

They swung left, crossing the hill into the trees with difficulty, hanging onto whatever grew handy, and once

Alex fell when a seven-foot horseweed came up, roots and all. He got up grinning, picked up the shaft, defoliated it, and hefted it. Aiming the rooty end, he sent it spear-fashion up onto the hill, into the backyard. It would dry quickly, and even Andy and Alex's wife Deb enjoyed playing with the hollow segments of stalk. (Deb was a product of the sixties, when everyone in the country was naming children Kevin and Debbie and Jeffrey. There were more Kevins in the United States now than there had been in Ireland in the last hundred and twenty years, someone calculated, and someone else said that had the people of Biblical times been as mad about the name Deborah as mid-twentieth-century America there'd have been the story of Deborah and Naomi, Deborah Magdalene, and the Blessed Virgin Deborah. As to all the Jeffs; Chaucer would have frowned over the new spelling, and Jeff Andrews was ridiculously proud that his name was Jefferson, not Jeffrey, and after Thomas J., not J. Davis.)

The branch running down the hollow between tree-choked hill and backyard was nearly dry. There hadn't been rain for six days. The tree frogs were wherever they betook their pale selves when things became too dry for them to spend all night cheering and singing the virtues of falling water.

'That oak's stranglin' the sassafras, Jeff,' Alex said.

Jeff regarded the straggly sassafras, then tilted back his head to study the big chinquapin beside it.

'Chink's got another ten-fifteen years in it, Alex. Let's leave 'em. There's more trees concentrated right here than there are in what's left of the Dannel Boone National Forest.'

'I reckon.'

'Let's let Mister sassy-frass fight to exist. He's no better'n we are.'

'I reckon not.'

'Time is it?'

Alex glanced up. He seldom bothered with his watch, when he was out. He always wore long sleeves with the cuffs buttoned, August or December, and he never rolled the sleeves up, either. Glancing at the sky was easier than peeling back his left cuff to his watch.

''Bout 'leven.'

'Let's be heroes and go weed a little.'

'Unh. Jeff?'

'Yeah.' Jeff was climbing the little acclivity into the backyard. He hung onto a branch until he felt Alex's hand on it, so that it wouldn't fly back and switch the other man. Then he swung on up.

'Jeff, wha'd you plant last night?'

'Alex, you are entirely too goddam observant. How'd you know?'

'Eyes,' Alex said, coming up beside him. They stood beside the last of the Japanese irises – all "flags" to Alex. As yellow jonquils were March flares, meaning flowers.

'Yeah, well. You and those damned eyes.' Jeff grinned at him. 'Who else knows?' He squinted at the Kentucky coffee tree. He hoped it thrived this year. Bitter home-roasted coffee was preferable to sassafras tea, any day.

Alex said nothing. It wasn't worth answering. He *told* no one anything. Alex's concept of the human vocal chords was that they had been provided for the sole purpose of answering questions. And not always then; the mere incidence of a question's being asked was not to Alex sufficient reason to mandate his replying. Some things're obvious.

'OK,' Jeff said. 'It uz a man. Andy 'n I found 'im on the wire. Figured he c'd be of use to us. Planted 'im last night.'

'Twicet?'

'Nope.' Jeff was making a cigarette, careful not to spill any of the tobacco. The tobacco they traded for with Gary Bowen, over on the hill across the big road. Gary had very little of the one strange commodity Jeff still received from his agent in New York: money. Nobody used it a hell of a lot, but it was still a good trade item.

'Nope, I buried 'im four times. In four places, I mean.'

'Gawd.'

'Yeah, well, he'll be good for the greenery, next year.'

'I reckon. Recycle. Know 'im?'

'Nope. Never saw 'im. Had a thirty-ought-six and a .38 revolver, snubby. I put 'em away.'

'Like to teach Deb to handle a .38. Think she's got the weight for it, now.'

'Yeah, and she's death on wheels with that .32. OK, we'll buy a box of cartridges next time we go to town. Gonna have to go within the next few weeks, anyhow. Got to replace that pipe, and the list is gettin' long. You know how Josie is about spices.'

Alex smiled his quiet smile. He began rolling a cigaret after Jeff did, finished it first and handed the match to the other man. Jeff lit up and performed his death-to-fire ritual.

'I'n use some blades, too,' Alex said.

Jeff glanced at him. Alex shaved every day. It wasn't quite the way of his daddy and his daddy's daddy, who had often let it go through the week, shaving on Saturday night before visiting the bootlegger. And looking mostly clean-shaven for preacher, Sunday noon. But Alex was a step above them, education and pride and job, and he had made that a part of his status. (He'd been an electrician.) Daily shaving. Now that he had returned, with Jeff, to the life of his great-great-great granddaddy, he retained the custom. Along with long-sleeved shirts, buttoned. Unless of course he was doing heavy sunwork, in which case he often stripped to the waist and was deeply tanned in a day. He never burned. As if it were all as he believed, as his people believed: god had put the sun here, and god had put man here, and they were supposed to get along.

Jeff had started letting his beard grow when he sold his fifth novel, the one he got three thousand for (back when that was enough to buy, say, a VW), along with a 6 percent contract. After that he'd kept it, shaving his neck and his upper cheeks and clipping his mustache and beard with an expensive pair of scissors. It was a symbol, of course, and no one had mistaken him for a Hippie or a Dovey. Ten years ago he had ceased shaving altogether, and merely trimmed it daily with scissors as always, and about once a month with an old electric razor. Josie's. That it was pink did not disturb him in the least. He'd been sure of his manhood early on, somehow, which made him a most unusual man, particularly in America.

He and Alex were about as much alike as last year's peas and this year's, the red ones. They both loved trees, and wandering around over the property. But Alex had that innate genius with machinery and mechanical contrivances of all kinds, from bicycle sprockets to the basement generator. Jeff was a mechanical illiterate; his goal for years had been to be able to afford all sorts of the machinery that fascinated him, and to be able to afford to pay someone to fix it. He and Josie had a long-standing joke that either she had to replace light bulbs or stand by to read him the written instructions while he did.

Light bulbs were what you used to use for lighting, short-lived vacuum chambers that had improved hardly at all from Edison's first one to the Westinghouse of the late seventies. They were collectors' items, now. Jeff had two, and an old no-deposit no-return bottle, too, on which he had once painted, in anger, a bright red skull and crossed bones. He even kept the old Mercedes, with its gasoline engine, a triumph of inefficient propulsion and atmospheric death that had lasted and lasted until it was outlawed. Not because of its ridiculous inefficiency, but because it spewed fumes so deadly people even used their automobiles to commit suicide in the garage in the old days.

He didn't drive it much now. He drove the Andretti, when he drove. Which was seldom.

The two men crushed their cigarets out, dead out, and went up to start weeding. But as they passed the back door Deb stuck her blonde head out.

'Jeff – telephone. It's Noah Hough.'

'Generator needs oil,' Alex muttered, following Jeff into the coolth of the house.

'Hey Noey! What's doing in the big city?'

'Recycle, Jeff. Hired two more police this week. And Council voted to stop fire protection to North Wilson Avenue.'

'Damn! Tough on them – how many police is that now, Noey?' Jeff parked his rump on a stool at the breakfast bar, hunching his shoulder to hold the phone while he reached for his tobacco. Then he realized he'd just had one. He wished he hadn't. Cigarettes were telephone things.

'A hundred and forty-one,' Noah said. 'Bob over at the paper says there were about ten in seventy, counting the ones at the college.'

'Know what the population was then, Noey?'

'Uhyeah. Bout five thousand, plus six thousand students, except in August. Now they's about twenny thousand.'

'Took ten cops for eleven thousand and a hundred and forty for twenty thou, huh? Listen Noey, you city people are gettin' just mean as hell, you know?'

Noah chuckled, 'Yeah – can't blame it on the students anymore, either.'

Jeff laughed; it was a politeness.

'What's goin' awn out there in the sticks, Jeff?'

'Nothing much. Zapped a ripper last night; spread the word, will you? Like to keep people shook up about comin' around here. This isn't a good place for a rip-off. Oh, and we seem to be raising red peas.'

'Unyeah, red peas; Adrian told me 'bout them yesterday. They're all over the county. Ag Department says they're OK to eat.'

'Sure they are, Noey. Everything's GOOD for us. Listen, Josie says it's goin' to be pretty funny, seeing ads for the Jolly Red Giant.'

Noah laughed; it was more than a politeness. 'Good, good. Give me somethin' to tell all day, Jeff. Listen, Jeff, when you comin' in?'

'Come on, Noey, you scamp, that's no fair. Whatcha got?'

'Airmail envelope from Jake Wilson in New York City.'

'Fat?'

'Skinny.'

'Open it up, Noey?'

'Oh my gracee-yoss, Mister Andrews sir, that's against the postal regulations. You don't think the Yew Ess Postmaster's goin' to open yer *mail*, do you?'

'Yep. Open 'er up, Noey.'

Jeff listened to the sound of the ripping envelope. He knew Noah always held the envelope near the phone when he tore it open, so Jeff could hear it and know it had remained sealed until Noah called him and they went through their ritual. Noah always called about mail from Jeff's agent; Jeff always had Noah open it.

'Hey, whatchou been writin' this time, Jeff?'

'Biography of ole Noah Hough, what else. What is it, damn you?'

'Two vouchers and a note. Want to hear the note? Says "Memo from Jake Wilson." '

'The checks, Noey, you damned possum-smiling runt.'

'You country folks sure are impatient, Jeff. Ought to lead a nice quiet life like us townies. By the way, Bishop's got ripped off last night.'

'Get 'em?'

'Naw. The rippers uz from Off. Got em at the Mount Sterlin's exit. They wouldn't stop, so the Mount Sterlin' police put a bazooka through the car.'

'That sure as hell stopped 'em, but it didn't get Dan Bishop much of his own back, did it?'

'Nope. Jeff, one voucher's for thirty-five hundred,' Noah said, his voice dropping as if his volume had been turned from nine to one on a scale of ten. Jeff knew he was glancing around, making sure no one heard. 'Other'n's for three-thirty-two-twenny-nine. Note says Jake's sorry, he did a bookkeeping screwup and took his commission out of the royalty money from Star Press and the other one's the full advance from Bobby Merrill for "Ecologesis." What's that?'

'Word I made up. Bobbs-Merrill, Noey, right?'

'Says Bobby Merrill, Jeff. B-O-B-B-Y. . . .'

'OK, sorry. Jake never could type worth a shit. Will you take 'em over to the bank for me, Noey?'

'Already in. These're vouchers. Wilson just made an account transfer. You're loaded, Jeff.'

'Thanks, Noah. That about it?'

'Yeah, aside from five packages of books and about

eighty-five magazines and a few dozen letters. When you comin' in, Jeff?'

'Pretty soon, Noey. Thanks.'

'Jeff, it's no big deal to come into town. 'Sonly eight miles. Don't see you enough. We uz talkin' 'bout you thother night. Lord, they's no danger in drivin' in from your place to town, not on Rowan County highways.'

'You're right, Noey. I'm just a damned recluse,' Jeff said, thinking of the eighty or ninety bad things that could happen to him on the way to town, in town, and to his family as soon as someone spotted him in town and decided to try a daylight rip.

'Well, gotta go now, Jeff. Recycle. Come see me.'

'Recycle, Noey, and be careful,' Jeff said, and they hung up. He grinned at Deb, who was making an elaborate pretense of not-listening while she sat three feet away, peeling potatoes. He rushed upstairs, slapped Josie on the fanny, and told her they'd just gotten four thousand dollars richer.

She hugged him. 'That OK a Sears order?'

'That sure and hell OK's a Sears order,' He said. 'Put it together and we'll phone it in. Ought to get here in a week, and I'll plan on going into town next week.'

Josie nodded, sighing a little. She hadn't been off the hill in two years. Not since Janie.

Chapter Four

Morehead really hadn't changed much, Jeff Andrews thought.

Sure, the population had doubled since seventy, after remaining static – except for the students – for decades. Actually it hadn't doubled but quadrupled, if you took into account the fact that in the sixties and seventies half the populace vanished every August, when the university shut down for a month between the post summer and fall sessions.

But it really hadn't changed much. Back then it had been a tiny town whose major industry was the university. Now, with four times as many permanent residents, it was still tiny. The dormitories, along with most of the classroom buildings, had become apartments. (Those that hadn't been burned before universities were closed.) Morehead was still sleepy, and quiet, and Main Street still was, although now it was several miles longer. And it was still dry, which Jeff still thought was funny.

Kentucky, land of fast horses and beautiful women (fast women and beautiful horses, Kentuckians said, and always laughed dutifully at the joke born time out of mind); Kentucky, where the Derby had a bad habit of being won by horses from other states.

Kentucky, land of the long rifle – defeated in six out of the final eight long-rifle meets by the Pennsylvanians, D. Boone fit a b'ar here or not.

Kentucky, home of the bluegrass – which was nearly all gone down in the bluegrass section, now, since Lexington had moved out west to encompass Versailles (Ver-SALES, and sometimes VER-sales), and north to envelop Paris, and south to Nicholasville, and east two-thirds of the way to Winchester – which grew out to meet it. The bluegrass had given way to concrete. People who wondered what it was and thought it was a myth would never know what bluegrass had been: tall and wavy and snakeskin blue in the sunlight.

Jeff Andrews had a backyard full of it, and it bordered the road, too. But something had happened to it. It didn't glint that cold, hard blue anymore in the July sun; what there was of the July sun that showed.

Kentucky, land of bourbon whiskey. Stitzel-Weller and Beam and Dant, Old Grandad and Old Fitzgerald and Maker's Mark and JTS Brown and Old Heaven Hill and Old Bardstown and . . . so many others, all made in the state, in the main around the monstrous sprawling octopus that had been the little river town Louisville, and down in the Catholic country of Fairfield and Bardstown and Springfield, near Loretto and Lebanon Junction and just outside Lancaster. Home of bourbon whiskey, with 120 counties – ruled by JP's and county judges and magistrates – and when Jeff was growing up, over nearer Louisville before he moved east to Morehead in the Appalachian foothills, precisely nine of those counties had been wet. Many Kentuckians had to drive a long way to get their state's noblest product since tobacco could not be termed noble. Oh sure, there were the bootleggers.

Jeff's favorite bootlegger had been the Drivearound. He wondered if it were the country's only drive-in boot; he hoped so. It didn't matter how old you were, so long as you had the (inflated) price and someone knew you. That part was made a little difficult by the fact that the 'leggers were raided consistently. Especially in election years. Particularly in August and September and October, before election day in November – when thousands of half-pints were passed out all over the state in return for a promised vote, because that was the way things were done and rural Kentuckians didn't break promises. But every time there was a raid the owners of the county's most popular businesses had had to bring in new clerks, and many more times than once Jeff had driven in to be greeted by a strange face.

'Gimme six tall ones,' Jeff had said from the car, because he didn't believe in paying exalted prices for liquor; he bought that in Mt. Sterling or Lexington, which became very close once the Interstate was completed to within four or so miles of Morehead.

And he'd been greeted by an impassive face, the flat eyes of the blacksnakes Kentucky farmers cherished in an innate sense of ecology; blacksnakes had a natural liking for mice, which had a natural hankering for corn.

'Don't believe I know ye,' the mouth below the flat eyes would say. (Giving him the old jaundiced eye, Jeff's neighbors said, only partially accepting him because he was after all from Off, and west at that, and he'd be a Johnny-come-lately for another hundred years or so, provided he tried real hard; otherwise he'd be a J-C-L all his life and so would his children.)

'You're new,' Jeff said. 'Don't believe I know you either. I'm Jeff Andrews.' And he would ease up his left buttock and pull out his wallet and pass it over. 'Check that, then look right there over your head, right above the window.'

The clerk, often shirtless because the tin-roofed little building was hot – refrigeration was for beer – would accept the wallet and check the driver's license and the People's Bankamericard and scan the Kentucky Colonel card without being impressd – only out-of-staters were – all in his own time. Then he would lift his eyes to the little notation above the window. Jeff knew what it said.

'Jeff Andrews is ok. Serv him and maybe youl get in a book.'

The clerk would pass the wallet back, never having glanced into the money compartment. He was working regular and Andrews looked like he was, from the car. What he carried in the way of money was his business.

'Six tall Buds,' the clerk would say, nodding, and disappear shirtless to return with six pint cans of cold Bud in a brown paper sack, already closed. No one ever checked. One thing about bootleggers; they were honest. And Jeff passed over his two one-dollar bills.

Jeff had never patronized the Clock, on the road the other end of town. For a while, when the price war was going on, they passed out a nickel bag of Tom's potato chips or corn curls, your choice, with every purchase, even the staple: half pints of Abie's Wild Irish Rose wine. But the Drivearound was on Jeff's way home from town, and he liked the place. It was convenient.

Then some damned fool bastard had got serious about the law, and within two months the local State Police barracks had raided bootlegger after bootlegger, time after time. They had broken the code, the old code that the 'leggars were just raided now and again so there could be pictures in the paper and a candidate for magistrate or county judge or whatever could say he was trying to protect Rowan County's kids from the evils of strong drink. And suddenly Rowan County was very very dry, shocking those of Jeff's friends and acquaintances who – in those days – still came up from Lexington or even Louisville now and then.

'The charm of bootlegging,' Jeff Andrews had said more than once and finally put into a novel, 'and the charm of places like the Drivearound, is equivalent to the charm of Lincoln's birthplace and My Old Kentucky Home over in Bardstown. We should protect them the same way. I'd like to see the Drivearound turned into a public shrine, if it must be closed down, with a half-full freezer and a snake-eyed wax clerk standing in the window and a car standing just outside, its ass end dragging the ground because it's just come up from Mount Sterling with a trunkful of good Kentucky booze.'

But he'd driven to Lexington or Mount Sterling after that, like everyone else. He began to go in conjunction with the arrival of novel checks, and then novel vouchers when banking changed and checks went out and a man couldn't engage in a little kiting in the final week of the month anymore. In Mount Sterling he bought three or four bottles at a time, and a couple of dozen cans of beer. In Lexington he bought cases; Lexington's prices were lower. It wasn't a last outpost to places like Morehead and Owingsville and West Liberty, the way Mount Sterling was.

Morehead was still dry, and Jeff was thinking about the old days with the 'leggars as he pulled into the Town Garage on the eastern outskirts. He and Andy got out; it was Andy's turn to come with him.

'Yes, sir,' the boy said, a new boy since Jeff's last visit to town. 'You folks want a minik?'

Andy's eyes lit; Jeff shook his head. 'Think we'll walk.'

'How about a coupla bicycles? Got three of the new ones, the ones with—' A plane shattered the sound barrier overhead and they all stood shaking. The boy cursed, cupping a hand over the left side of his chest.

'Think we'll just walk,' Jeff said. Alex would have said 'reckon' rather than "think", Jeff said it, too, when he remembered.

'I'll need your driver's license and bank – yes, thank

you. Hey – I've heard of you. Hi, Mr. Andrews. I've heard of you.'

Jeff smiled at him. ''Preciate it,' he said. 'Quit hearin' of me and start gettin' my books, will you? I need the money.'

He'd been saying it for years, and for years people had been laughing, just as the boy laughed now. He handed back the bank ID and Jeff's license.

'I'll do that, I swear I purely will do that,' the youngster said, very thin and maybe about Andy's age. 'Have fun in Morehead, Mr. Andrews.'

'My son Andy,' Jeff said.

'Recycle,' the boy said. 'I'm Buford Holly.'

'Take care of that car, Buford Holly,' Jeff said, and he and Andy commenced walking into town.

Within a quarter of a mile they were stopped by a local police car. Jeff didn't recognize the two men inside.

'You fellas live around here?'

'Name's Jeff Andrews,' Jeff told the one with the florid face under the visored white helmet. 'I own, out to Haldeman. This's my son Andy. You're some of the new policemen Noey at the post office told me about.'

Name-dropping; these two didn't call Noah by his first name, and Jeff knew it. Noah was on the town council, and owned a piece of the DairyFreez. Not to mention the piece of land the post office occupied.

'Oh yeah, Mr. Andrews, heard of you,' the two policemen agreed, nodding and smiling. 'Want a ride into town?'

Jeff laughed. 'Look pretty bad, me riding into town in the back of that, wouldn't it?'

The skinny one looked hurt; Florid-face grinned and shrugged, swinging his foot back into the armored prowl car. 'Now no one would think a thing about it, not a thing, from what I hear about you.'

Jeff couldn't resist asking what the man had heard about him.

'Law-abidin' prop'ty-owner, minds his own business and keeps his place in a sacred stewardship, never did a mean thing in his life, nice guy unless you cross him, got a way with words makes you sit there after he leaves and wonder if you should've shot him.'

Jeff laughed. The man was honest enough. 'Want to ride into town, Andy?'

'Sure.'

They climbed into the back of the prowl car, Andy's eyes roaming swiftly about, flitting over the car's interior like a hummingbird's wings.

'Who told you all that stuff about kindly, peaceable old Jeff Andrews?' Jeff asked, as the car moved slowly into town.

'Oh – everybody. Never read anything by you, though. What do you write about?'

Jeff was used to it. He didn't know who in hell read his books and occasional short stories, but it certainly wasn't anyone in Rowan County. Of course even now with a population of better than twenty thousand there was no bookstore, but after all – the drugstores carried paperbacks, and he had given the library two of everything, paperbacks and cloth alike.

'Lotta bull,' Jeff told him. 'What else is there to write about?'

'Name's Gaddie,' the policeman said, raising his helmet to scratch his sweat-damp hair. 'Omer Gaddie.'

'Used to know some Gaddies, over in Spencer County,' Jeff said.

'No kin, I reckon. They's a lot of Gaddies in Kentucky, and over in West Virginia, too, Dad says. Got some good stories in the old family, too. You ought to write about us Gaddies.'

'Maybe I will,' Jeff said, because it was what he always said. Everyone had good stories, and had always wanted to write them down, and since you're a writer maybe I could tell you some stories and you'd write it up the way it ought to be and get it published, mother (dad/uncle) would like that. 'Who's your strong silent partner?'

The skinny driver laughed. 'Name's John Quesenberry,' he said. 'Everybody calls me just Pip, though.'

'Well, the next time I get a chance to put a couple of darned nice lawmen in a book,' Jeff said, 'I'll just name them Pip Gaddie and Omer Quesenberry.'

'Pip GADDIE!'

'Omer Quesenberry!'

Jeff was ostentatiously making a note of both names. He nodded without looking up. 'Sure. I'll be darned if I put your real exact names in there. You two guys might decide to sue me.'

Everybody laughed, and Andy wanted to know what this was, and Pip told him careful, touch that and it grabs your hand, and he showed Andy the steering-wheel stud that dropped the iron curtain between front seat and rear.

'Not all our passengers are as nice and willin' as you and your daddy,' Pip said. 'We've been using solid curtains instead of that link fence stuff ever since Chief Kirk got it in the back from a guy he picked up, ten-twelve years ago. I mean, I wasn't on the Force then, but that's when City Council started in using solid screens.'

'Had any trouble out your place, Mr. Andrews?'

'Call me Jeff, Omer, you make me feel like an old man. Yeah, or sort of. Fellow got himself killed on my hill a few nights ago. How about getting out your little book and writing it down now, so Andy and I won't have to go to the station? I don't want to have to do *too* much messin' around with police when I'm in town.'

Omer laughed and rummaged in the instrument panel slot that was still called a glove compartment. 'OK,' he said.

'Well, I've got some defenses I won't go into. . . .'

'Oh, yeah, Mist – Jeff, please don't. I don't want to know about a man's personal property defense systems,' Omer said, spewing out the words he'd learned in police school and making them sound alien to his lips.

'OK. Well, he ran onto a little something I've got rigged out there, and Andy and I found him next morning. He was dead.'

Making quick notations, Omer Gaddie nodded. 'Uh-huh. What'd you do with 'im?'

'Planted 'im,' Jeff said.

Omer looked up, twisting his neck. 'Now that's what I call dern Christian of you, Mi – Jeff.'

Jeff smiled. 'Not really. I didn't read any words over him.'

'And he's good for the garden,' Andy said, playing callous.

'Reckon so. Was he from round here?'

'Nuh-uh. Name was Michael Kissel, from Lexington.'

'Oh Lord, *Lexington!* That's where they're all from. Well, we'll send this on down to them, uh, Jeff, and that'll be it I expect. Never saw 'im before?'

'No. He was carrying a rifle and a pistol.' Jeff nodded at the gun on Andy's hip. 'That's it.'

'Nice gun,' Omer said. 'I'll bet you can use it too, huh?'

Andy nodded, looking tough. 'When I have to,' he said, which Jeff recognized as a line from a movie. Funny; there'd always been a lot of Westerns on the theater screens and on television, back when men went unarmed and longed for the men-were-men days of the instant trial and scabbard justice. Now that the country had nearly returned to those days, cowboys remained just as popular. More. These days people took notes.

Man never got enough of instant "justice" and killing, Jeff thought, and repeated it in his brain. Someday he'd try to write about Andy; the line would belong in that book. He glanced at the boy – was a fellow a boy when he was taller than his father and wore a gun? He wondered. If he raped someone, the newspaper called him a man. If he was in service, he was a boy. They all were, Our Boys in Service.

Andy was paying no attention to anything, now, except what he saw outside the car. People, Female people.

Even the new shoe-top skirts made them look female, Jeff thought. There was no mistaking the shape of a feminine bottom, feminine hips, no matter what she wore or didn't wear.

Andy kept up his looking, all day. He got some looks in return, plenty of them. He wasn't a towny, that was obvious and somehow they knew, instinctively, that he wasn't a "standard" farmer, what usually came in from the sticks. Besides, some of them recognized his father or their mothers did, and there was no mistaking Jeff's beard for an unshaven face.

Someone had laughingly called him a Gyppie once, Noah or Jack probably, and Jeff had shaken his head and said no, the difference between him and the old Hippies and Yippies and the new Gyppies was that he had a beard; they just didn't shave.

Jeff did some buying and some visiting, and Andy did a lot of staring. In the bank, while Jeff transacted business and visited, Andy stared at a pretty teller with long black hair.

On the street outside, Jeff told him, 'Got to watch the hands, son. She was wearing a wedding ring.'

'Who?'

'Uh-huh.'

'Well, she sure was lookin' back,' Andy said, dropping the pretense.

'Some women do,' Jeff said, grinning, and eliciting a return smile from the girl they passed.

'Was that one married?'

'Didn't notice,' Jeff said, glancing back to watch the wobble of the girl's backside and meeting her eyes as she glanced back to watch the wobble of his, or something.

'Uh-huh,' Andy said.

Sure, Jeff thought, I'll just make some arrangements with Noah and Roger and some others. We'll have another party out at the house, and this time it'll be bring-your-unmarried-younguns too. Andy'll have one picked by midnight, and surely no one would object to his daughter's getting the hell out of town!

There'd been a lot of parties out at the house. So long as the guests came together, there was no worry about trouble, either en route or on the way back to town. People in town understood why Jeff and Josie no longer came in to parties, or dances, or anything else. Pike Willett had been in town on a Wednesday night, attending prayer meeting with his younger son and daughter, when his place had been visited by Gyppies, just four years ago. His wife and son had killed four of the motorcycle gypsies, but that hadn't been enough. Pike had returned home after having done what he thought was right by his kids and incidentally making the preacher happy, and he'd found a scene so ugly no one ever talked about it. A year later, three years ago, Pike had left the kids in town while he took off to somewhere or other, and a month or two after he came back word got around that he had a woman. A woman from Off, a city woman. No one knew whether he'd kidnapped her or not, but she was happy enough to stay, everyone noticed. Everybody in Lexington would surely want to live in Morehead, which was sure safer and quieter because it was smaller, and all cityites hated land-people because they envied them. (Maybe not all of them did, but some people were born crazy and there's no accounting for tastes.)

So they understood why Jeff and Josie didn't leave the place at night, and why Josie didn't leave it at all, and they understood, too, why Andy stared at their daughters and even their wives.'

'How old is he, Jeff?'

'Eighteen, Noey.'

'What's'e goin' to do?'

'Do? Live. Keep the place. Stay there, of course.'

'He's gonna be an oddun, Jeff. No people around, no girls, nothin' that's normal.'

'What's normal, Noah?' Jeff was rolling a cigarette. Andy was across the street at Bishop's, enjoying a fountain Coke. And the view.

Noah waved a hand. 'Don't be obtuse, Jeff. You know what I mean.'

'Sure, I know. Normal is you live in a city, like New York. You marry a girl you meet at work, or somebody who lives in the same apartment building, because you don't go anywhere else. You don't care. Normal is three couples going out together, for protection, and getting attacked by ten or twenty. Normal is the girls get raped and the boys get killed, and if they don't the Feps come along and maim or kill or run them all in anyhow, indiscriminately. Normal is England, dying, awallow in a tepid and scum-coated sea of socialism and roaming gangs worse than our Gyppies. Normal is Japan, dominating most of the Pacific and half of China, and changing its birth laws in occupied territory while holding to a one-per-family-or-you-get-shot rule at home. Normal was last week's news: the government's letting contracts to build still *another* block of high-rises in the Dannel Boone National Forest.'

'Hey, Jeff. Man, you are gettin' rabid.'

'I am LIVING, Noah, and I'll bet meat there's someone in a city, someone right here in town, who thinks *he's* living and I'm crazy. One of us is maybe right and one maybe wrong, and maybe we're both right.'

'Or both wrong.'

Jeff nodded. 'Or both wrong. *Normal*! Normal is the New York City crisis-of-the-month-club getting "solved" by Operation Food-drop. Thousands and thousands of pounds of food on parachutes coming down, collapsing early so they didn't make the buildings look like Christmas trees. Which meant everyone was down in the streets grabbing. A hundred and fifty thousand killed in the rush for the food, isn't that the figure? And for what? The Panthers got it anyhow, and they're selling it back to the people – for their guns and their daughters and lord knows what else. And only about two-thirds of the Panthers are black.' He shook his head. 'That's one way to integrate, anyhow.'

'And one way to get rid of the Mafia,' Noah said.

'Yeah. The Mafioso hasn't been born who's a match for a gang of Panthers or Gyppies or Doveys or you-name-its, young people with one brain: pure wolf.'

'OK, Jeff. But about Andy—'

'Yeah, about Andy. And Kristy, too. And then Scott. He's sixteen. Noey. Remember dates? How many dates had you had by the time you were sixteen?'

Noah leaned back grinning, wagging his head. 'Ha! A bunch! I had my first piece when I was thirteen. She's still living rightcheer in town, too. But not with me, not with me!' He gazed at the wall past Jeff's head for a time, grinning and letting his mind wander back. Jeff could see it moving back, ever backward, that brain, as everyone's did.

The good old days were the sixties and seventies, the worst and most hideous decades, the most barbarous times in the history of the nation and the world. Up till then.

'Oh,' Noah said, his eyes dropping to Jeff's again. 'Did you hear about yesterday? Most of Chattanooga's gone. Nobody even knows how it happened. Eighty or ninety million in property damage; about a hundred thousand people killed or nearly.'

'I heard,' Jeff said. 'Listen, about Andy—'

MEANWHILE: II

A City Is A Great Place to Live, But I'd Hate to Have to Live *in* It

'Pass the salt, Jake,' Harry Loschke said, and Jake Wilson broke up. He made elaborate movements of his arm and hand, swinging it up toward the vizer; Harry, just as elaborately, raised his hand on Jake's screen and pretended to accept the saltcellar he had palmed.

'Remember the last time I passed you the salt, Harry? Really, I mean.'

'Sure I do. Lunch at Duff's, from twelve-fifteen until four in the afternoon, and you introduced me to that girl only got turned on by giving head. Sure I remember, Jakey.'

Jake cut off another piece of steak. His was soybean, but Harry didn't have to know that. It looked just like the one Jake had had delivered to Harry, after paying twenty-one fifty for it and crossing his fingers that the Panther with Brother Nathaniel on his black jacket wouldn't just go over the hill with it. Brother Nathaniel hadn't; he had made delivery of both the steak and the twenty-dollar bottle of Jim Beam to Harry's, and Jake and Harry were having another of many business lunches.

'And the next day I bought three novels,' Harry said. 'Would you accept it, Jake, I hadn't even *read* one of them?'

Jake looked at his image on the screen. 'Did you lose money, Harry?'

'Jake, it pains my sweet ass to admit it, but I never lost money on a book I bought from you, whether you sold me or bribed me or blackmailed me.'

'Harry!'

'Shit, Jake, we have gotten old together. We are a pair of overmoneyed dinosaurs, and we've got that way together. Good grass, I remember when you decided you were going to be a literary agent, and you got me and Max and – what was his name, the guy got killed in the Battle of Detroit?'

'Nunnally. Nice boy. Lotta promise. Mighta made a writer, if he hadn't had those big ideas about justice and brotherhood. That's the only reason he decided to let me agent him, I think. If I'd been a WASP he'd have told me to go to hell, he'd find a black agent or a kike agent or whatever. A Pole, maybe.'

Harry chuckled. Made a toasting gesture with a forkful of steak so beautiful it made Jake want to cry.

'Who rewrote that first book of mine, Jake?'

Jake shook his head. 'Professional trust,' he said, laying a hand over his heart and smiling.

'Professional my sweet ass. Was it Gould?'

'It was not Gould.'

'Strauss?' Harry cocked his head. 'Was it that little blonde sex writer Cinthy Strauss?'

'It was not Cinthy. And stop calling her a sex writer. Her last mystery sold a hundred thousand in a year. You should have published it.'

'You should have sent it to me. Was it Maslow? Come on, Jake, I am old and may be ripped off and raped tonight by a gang of eight-foot Gyppies. Tell the old man who rewrote his first novel.'

'How do you feel about the Fischer book, Harry?'

'I feel like twenty-five hundred, Jake, and four and six.'

Jake shook his head. 'Thirty-five, Harry, and six and eight.'

'Jake, honest to god, it'll break me. This Fischer no one knows from an eight-ball.'

'It's a good book, Harry, and you know it.'

Harry sighed and reached for his milk. 'Jake, I swear—' He looked up swiftly. 'Three against four and six.'

'Three thousand dollars against six and eight, Harry, and we might be able to part with the book. With no reworking, which it doesn't need anyhow.'

'You are a monster, Jake Wilson, a monster. Your

mother would hate you. I'll bet you are secretly a Panther, and rape nice Jewish girls every night in the park.'

'The PARK!'

Harry waved a hand. 'The alley, the alley. I'm getting old, Jake. Since how long was there a park?'

Jake shrugged. 'Since years. And I spit on the Panthers. And I haven't dealt with Jews either – except for a few transactions now and then. And you know damned well I haven't been out of this apartment in eleven years, Harry you schmuck.'

'Sure, I know, I know. Fortified like a castle too, huh? It's a great city to live in, but I'd hate to have to live *in* it. So who rewrote my first book?'

'Why is that such a big thing today, Harry? So what's it matter who wrote your first book better than you did, which was very bad indeed? I sold it, and the next one too, and you got a job editing read-'em and beat-'em books, and look at you now. So fat you can't see your shoes.'

Grunting, Harry leaned back, twisted away from his table, and raised a leg. He waggled his toes at Jake Wilson. 'So who wears shoes? I just want to know, Jakey. Before I die, I want to know. I swear on my mother's grave I will never tell anyone. And three thou on the Fischer book, which is a first novel and may break me so that I become a garink.'

'And a 6 percent contract, Harry, and 90 percent of everything else.'

'What's the everything else? Who can sell foreign rights when every country hates every other country? Who's making movies, when people can't go out in groups of more than twenty without being subject to arrest? So all right.'

'Jeff Andrews rewrote your first book, Harry.'

'Jeff Andrews! Son of a bitch – how did that guy know so much to improve it?'

'He's a writer, Harry. You're an editor. You didn't know it then, but you are an editor. I helped you find out, remember?'

'You'll never let me forget – what about a brandy, Jake?'

'A brandy, yes,' Jake said. 'But you'll have to go out for it. Use my numbers.'

Harry sighed. 'A bourbon and water, then,' he said, reaching across his table so that his hand grew to Brobdingnagian proportions on Jake's screen. They poured a bourbon and water, each of them, and extended the glasses to their vizers. The glasses seemed almost to touch on the screens.

Harry drank, emitted a deep sigh, and leaned back with a cat-happy smile. 'Jeff Andrews. How many sexbooks did he write, Jake, while he was writing the good stuff that now makes us all money?'

'Dozens. You bought only a third of them, Harry. And changed every title.'

'Ah – I want to change this latest one, too. So what's *Ecologesis*? Say it out loud and it sounds religious.'

Jake laughed. 'Harry, it is a good title. Everyone knows what ecology means, now. It's a good word. It will attract some new buyers. Everybody knows what ecology is, Harry.'

Harry sipped some more bourbon and water, leaning back in his chair, peering at his friend on his screen. He lowered the glass.

'Yeah,' he said, 'we all know. And we know about breeding, too. And it's a strange book, a backward science fiction, showing what the country COULD have been like in 1980, which is the past, Jake, the past, for pete's sake.' He spread his hands, sloshing not a drop from the glass in his left. 'I think he can get away with a backward science fiction, Jake, but I am going to put his name on the cover in big white – no, yellow – letters and the title will be in letters a third so big.'

'I'm telling you, Harry—'

'Sure, sure, you're telling me. Everybody knows what ecology is. So how come we got so smart so late? So why didn't someone invent the word in nineteen hundred or whatever, instead of waiting until sixty-eight or whenever it was, when it was too late? I ask you.'

He gazed at Jake a moment, then glanced down at his watch. 'Hey, I've gotta go. Jake, it was fun, and you sold me another bill of goods, and thanks for the lunch. Go on back to the office.'

'Recycle, Harry.'

'Shit.' Harry's hand rose, growing in the screen, fingers curling to twist a knob. Harry vanished; Jake's screen blanked. He cut off his own vizer, smiled, and touched the button to start the cassette tape Jeff Andrews had sent him. Birdsongs filled the apartment, ringing back from the iron-screened windows.

Then Jake got up and walked into the other room: back to the office.

Chapter Five

Chuck Chaplin and his son Wayne rode down to Lexington with Jeff and Andy. Chuck had been a professor of math at the university, a department head, in point of fact. Now he lived on his Displaced Professors Fund income from the government, supplemented by the books he and Jack Payne labored over and sent out to be turned into ETV-C tapes. They drove Chuck's old gas-burner, which was acceptable on Interstates, provided it was garaged at Lexington's East Gate. They day-rented a minik to head in for Jeff's favorite liquor store. It was a shame to have to pay a day's rent on a vehicle they needed for an hour or so, but that was the only way the electric cars were rented, and Jeff would not set foot in any sort of public conveyance.

Making his own liquor was one thing Jeff wouldn't do. Many did now, even in the cities. Federal agents weren't out of jobs, they were just needed for other purposes in other places. Many had gotten honest work at last. For the first time in history the hills of Eastern Kentucky were full of unconcealed stills. The Property Protection Act and the Self-Defense Act made their operators even more stable than the lack of harassment by revenuers. The test case in Pike County thirteen years ago had settled that.

'Put up your hands, you're under arrest. We're Federal agents,' the five revenue men had said, and Arlis Hatfield had raised his hands, then fallen flat. That was when his wife Billie had opened up with the thirty caliber, and rid the country of five men whose kind had been the bane of Eastern Kentucky for many years. Arlis and Billie Hatfield were found not guilty by a jury of their peers, by reason of the aforementioned laws. The government had appealed, and Arlis and Billie had been found guilty in a Federal court. Another appeal, and another, and the Supreme Court agreed that the Property Protection Act and the Self-Defense Act gave all men an equal right under the law to protect life and limb and property, and that the agents in question might well have been disguised rippers, and Arlis and Billie went back to work supplying their friends and neighbors. And the revenue agents left them the hell alone. Hell, even Pikeville's resident FBI agent became a customer. You had to admire the independence of people such as Arlis and Billie Hatfield, although it seemed a bit unfair and contradictory of them to accept the Government guar. inc. to boot, since they were making an excellent income from the still(s; they became entrepreneurs with three sub-stills). But that, after all, was an old Eastern Kentucky tradition. Government was fool enough to give a man money for doing nothing, a man was entitled. It was almost sinful not taking it.

But Jeff Andrews didn't buy home brew. He bought a case of Rothschild's Napoleon, a case of Calvert's gin and several cartons of quinine water, three quarts of Jim Beam and one of California rum, and two gallons of Rhine Wine. It came to just over three hundred dollars, and the clerk and liquor store owner both helped him load it into their delivery truck. Chuck Chaplin bought a dozen bottles of this and that, and Jeff called Budget Rentacar to tell them he was leaving the minik – into which the four of them had just been able to cramp themselves – at the store.

At the third traffic light seven under-twenties came off the curb, looking mean, and approached the van. Instead of having its screens dropped in their faces, they found themselves eyeball-to-bore with four pistols. They went on across the street, trying to act as if that had been their intention all the time.

At the seventh traffic light they stopped behind a minik driven by a girl with a great deal of shiny blonde hair. Neither she nor the men in the van behind her thought about prearrangement until the two men who had stepped off opposite curbs converged on her car. One stood grinning at her, his little 200-watt defenser poised purposefully above her hood, while the other rapped at her window. The silent statement was obvious: open up for whatever we want or your engine gets zapped.

People were crossing the street; others were waiting for the light in their miniks, others were driving back and forth across the intersection. All ignored the daylight rip-in-progress. The girl didn't even sound her alarm siren to summon police. She was that scared and taken by surprise, and there wouldn't have been time anyway. Making the two toughs mad might well have brought the laser up at her windscreen rather than her engine compartment.

Jeff pulled his rifle up from between his legs and opened his door.

'Hey, god, don't—' the liquor-store driver began, but one of his four passengers was already swinging out, and the others were doing things with their pistols. He began to quiver, his eyes wide and rolling as he realized what terrible dangerous barbarians these country people could be.

Jeff couldn't get a leg-shot at the man with the little laser: the girl's hood concealed his body from the belt down. Crouching a little to angle the shot upward without threatening the cars waiting for the light on the other side of the intersection, Jeff aimed quickly and fired. The sound was drowned by that of the jet roaring over.

The arm holding the defenser jerked back violently. The little tube flew out into the street. The man spun once and a half and went down. His partner, just in the act of reaching into the car – the girl had opened her door – didn't even look at Jeff. He ran.

The light changed. The girl slammed her door. Her car lurched forward. The man writhing on the street looked up at the oncoming machine, tried to hurl himself out of the way. He didn't quite make it. The girl's car sent him flying and there was another loud bumping sound as his head bounced off the first car coming across the intersection from the opposite direction.

'You're welcome,' Jeff muttered, swinging back into the van.

'You – you—' the driver was unable to get it said, whatever it was. Horns began blowing. He started forward, killed his engine, started it and drove on. Traffic flowed around the mangled ripper. Now and again a tire nudged him or went over his hand; no one stopped.

'You people just would have let that happen, wouldn't you?' Andy asked.

The driver didn't say anything. He was scared. A man was usually pretty safe inside his car, particularly a big armoured delivery van. But he made it obvious he was not accustomed to sharing his mobile castle with out-of-town maniacs who played boy scout with guns.

He helped them transfer the liquor into Jack's car, then jumped into his van and raced away without waiting or even noticing the tip Jeff had ready.

Jeff stood staring after the departing vehicle.

'God,' he said.

'Is this the way things always are in the cities, Dad?' Andy asked.

'What was all that, Dad? – Mr Andrews?' Wayne asked.

'That,' Jeff said, sliding into Chuck Chaplin's car next to Jack, 'was civilization. Jack, let's get the hell back to those barbaric hills of ours.'

They did, at ninety-seven miles per hour; Chuck was careful to stay three miles below the speed limit. State troopers sometimes didn't bother trying to stop speeders; too many troopers had died that way. Too often now the clocker merely radioed ahead to the nearest roadside emplacement, and when the speeding vehicle passed it a couple of minutes later he got himself blown off the road. Those that survived were tried for speeding. The technique, coupled with the speed limit that had now been raised to reflect the realistic value of human life, was marvelously effective.

Jeff and Andy had a beer with Chuck and Joyce, transferred the liquor to their own car, and drove home. Their purchases in Morehead had just been delivered, seven hundred dollars' worth plus fifty for the eight-mile delivery. That included unloading, and of course operating an armored van with a driver and two guards wasn't an inexpensive operation. Morehead Delivery Inc. was making Lije Scutchfield a rich man, and people were beginning to forget he'd come to town only five years ago, from Off.

The news told them that there'd been a demo on the west side of Lexington, resulting in seven millions (estimated) in property damage and forty-one deaths. They hadn't even been aware of it, although it helped to explain why they'd seen so few policemen, down in the city.

Andy entertained them all at dinner with an only-slightly-embellished narrative of his father's heroism.

'What did she say?' Kris wanted to know. 'Was she pretty?'

Andy shook his head, smiling. 'She didn't even stop. We never saw her face. She didn't even turn around. I'll bet she juiced that car for all it had, all the way home.'

'Probably got picked up for speeding,' Jeff said quietly, gnawing on the knobby end of a legbone. He'd brought Arlie Eldridge salt for a couple of chickens and a dozen eggs, and chicken bones were worth cleaning. A fried chicken among eight people was more meat per person than most in India saw in a lifetime; more than most persons in cities saw in months, much less ate.

Josie was gazing at him, but not starry-eyed.

'Jeff, that wasn't . . . smart. You could have been killed.'

He nodded. 'Sure I could have been, but not by those two. I probably could have scared them off, too, without putting a bullet into him. But that *would* have been dangerous. The idiot might have tried to zap me and hit the van, or sapped that girl's car in a reflex jerk of his finger.'

'It wasn't your business,' Josie said.

'You're right. It wasn't. Nothing's my business. Certainly not some silly fluff-topped girl in Lexington who hasn't any more sense than to go out alone in a minik – and stop for a light when she's first in line.' He spread his hands. 'But how could I help it? There were five of us. FIVE, all male, and armed like a battalion. And there she was. I guess they wouldn't have raped her right there at the intersection. They'd probably just have got in and had her drive them someplace. Or maybe just ordered her out while they took off; maybe all they wanted was the car.'

He swallowed some coffee, home raised, home picked, home shelled, and home roasted. Kentuckians had been fortunate, in the days of the old Wilderness Road, for the existence of the Kentucky coffee tree. Now they were lucky for it again, with things the way they were in South America. Real coffee cost more than steak, and as few people in the nation tasted the one as the other.

'I couldn't help it,' he said again. 'If we hadn't been so well armed I probably wouldn't have done anything. I might have had to hold Andy back, but I would have. You don't go against weapons without weapons, and then only if you're good and you move fast. Besides, it all happened a lot faster and a lot less dramatically and herocially than Andy told it.' He glanced at his older son. 'Try writing it, son, the way you told it. Use other names. In other words spin a piece of fiction off that little scene. If it's any 'count we'll kick it around in the living room and send it up to Jake.'

Scott chewed his lip, studying his plate.

He wanted very much for Andy or Scot to write. Both of them played at it, but neither seemed to have the compulsion necessary to make a player with words into a writer. A lot of people wanted to be writers, but not to write, and a lot of people wanted to write, but not very much, not with discipline. He had hoped for years his own helpless compulsion would prove hereditary in at least one of his sons. As for his daughter . . . well, maybe, but Jeff Andrews was old fashioned. Sort of like the hounds they used to have. Josie fed them and the kids played with them. But they were Jeff's dogs. They came when Jeff appeared, they flopped and raised a hind leg to expose the genitals in a submissive gesture, they did what Jeff told them. Hounds, too, were old fashioned, true Southerners and true Eastern Kentuckians. Their world was based on men, a man. Women they tolerated. A hound was a hound, but if she were female she was invariably called "that little bitch". And everyone was astonished if she turned out to be worth a damn.

'Did you hear Glen Harvey on the car radio, Dad?' Kristy asked, sensing that the subject of her father's heroism (stupidity?) should be shelved.

'Sure didn't, babe. What'd he have to say today?'

'It was called Two Women,' Kris said, coaxing the sweet meat out of the crevices of her chicken-back. 'He showed them both, doing all the things they did and everything, and right away you saw it was a historical. You know, dinosaur-cars and filling stations, everywhere, those old-fashioned short skirts—'

'Minis,' Scott said.

'Minis're cars, dummy,' Roger said with considerable asperity.

'NOW they're cars,' Kristy told him. 'THEN they were skirts. Isn't that right?' She looked at her mother, of course. Josie nodded.

'Well,' Kristy went on, returning her gaze to her father, 'there were these two women. One had worked in a bank for twenty-one years. She made four-fifty-one a month, four *hundred* and fifty one, I mean, and Glen Harvey explained that that was about equivalent to eleven hundred now. And she had to travel to work and back every day, right downtown in a city, and she had to wear good clothes and have her hair done and all that, you know. It showed her working over her income tax and finally taking it to someone—'

'H.C. Block,' Roger supplied.

'H.R.,' Kristy nodded. 'Anyhow, she had to pay them to do her taxes for her, and she wrote them out a check, that was interesting, and mailed it and all. It showed her buying Christmas presents for her grandchildren and things – oh, she was a widow. Well – pass the salt, please – well, then they showed this other woman. She wasn't married, and she lived in another part of the same city. Not a very good section, you know. She had never been married, but she had five children. FIVE!'

'Monster,' Andy muttered automatically, Pavlovianly.

'And she didn't work. She had to stay home and take care of the children, of course.'

Andy was frowning. 'What did she do for money?'

'That's what it was all about,' Kris told him. 'She received five hundred and eleven a month from . . . ah, ADC. . . .'

'Aid to Dependent Children,' Jeff said.

Kristy nodded exuberantly, chewing rapidly, gulping to clear her mouth in order to speak. 'Yes yes, that's it, that's it. Aid to Dependent Children. The government. It was even before garink, I think. . . .'

Jeff answered the question in her eyes: 'Right.'

'Well, she got more money than the woman who worked, and who had had only two children too, in marriage, and was *making* money, by working. And not only that – oh, the first woman's name was Helen, the worker. The other one was Martha. Well, Martha got something called food stamps, too, and she could take those and get food for them, at the soupmarket. And she was . . . she was uh, actually like being married, *you* know, with this man who was the father of the children. He was unemployed, and he got money and food stamps, too, for not being employed.'

'Sounds crazy,' Andy said. 'Why didn't they get married?'

'Dammit son, we've talked about this. Remember the

causes of the Taxpayer's Revolt and the Working People's March on Washington and the Senate fight over recognition of the Poor People's Union of America?'

Andy frowned, chewing his lip. He nodded slowly. He jerked his head up to look at Kristy. 'They couldn't afford to get married!'

Kristy bobbed her head. 'Right, right. Because if they got married, she wouldn't have gotten her ADC money anymore, because the children would have had a father, and—'

'How can children not have a father, Daddy?' Roger wanted to know.'

Roger exchanged a look with Deb, who looked the other way. They pretended not to know about the wild things Jeff and Josie did in bed, too, and about the ancient and yellowed paperbacks they cherished up there in their bedroom.

'Your father will tell you later, Roger,' Deb said. 'Now hush and let Krissy finish her story.'

Despite the close proximity of their rearing, the Andrews children were considerably better informed and more talkative in some areas than Deb's and Alex's Roger. It came from parental attitudes and upbringing and education, and the fact that Alex and Deb were native born, while Jeff had, after all, brought Josie here from Off. Nor had he and Josie ever had the benefits of the religion of the mountains, glibly but best described as That Ole Time Religion.

'All children have fathers,' Kristy said. 'I mean if they'd got married the children would have had a *legal* father, right there, and that way the ADC wouldn't have paid Martha the money. And the seven of them couldn't have lived on what the father was getting from unemployment.'

'God, that was awful,' Andy said. 'Keeping them from getting married that way!'

'Oh, I don't know,' Alex said, and everyone looked quickly at him; Alex didn't talk all that much, and he joked even less. 'I'd say it was the same as being married, only better.'

'Well I like *that*,' Deb told him, aiming a *moue* at him.

'I kind of like it myself,' Jeff said.

'Hmp!' Josie's chin lifted. 'And just what have you been doing all day, Mr. Jefferson Andrews, ogling all the gals in Morehead and Lexington?'

He shook his head. 'There wasn't room on a one of them for my gaze to rest on,' he said, with more poetry than grammar. 'Andy's eyeballs were covering 'em all!'

Andy flushed, saying nothing. A moment later Jeff saw him frowning down at his plate. Scott was watching him.

'Anyhow,' Kristy said, 'at the end of the program Glen Harvey just sat there in that big chair of his and stared into the camera for about a minute. Then he said that next month the Congress would vote on whether to increase the money to the garinks, Guaranteed Income Incorporated has demanded another cost-of-living increase.'

Staring into his water glass, Jeff didn't say anything.

'Some day,' Alex said in his slow quiet way, 'Somebody's gonna kill Glen Harvey.'

Kristy smiled at her father. 'Not if Daddy's there they won't!'

MEANWHILE: III

A City Is A Helluva Place to Live, But I'd Hate To Be Mayor of One

. . . simple installation procedure insures you that your screens not only protect you against rippers, but may be hermetically sealed to assure you good clean air all day and night, from your own purification plant. Call your KleenSkreen man . . . TODAYYY.

And now here is Leonard Parrot with the news.

Hello, America, Leonard Parrot once again with a wrap-up of today's NEWS. First a look at the day's headlines, and then the news in depth after another word from Kleen-Skreen, your friend in deed.

Today's banner head:

(SUPERIMPOSED ON TV SCREEN AS PARROT INTONES)

MAYOR MEETS WITH MUGGER PRESIDENT

I'll have full details of that story for you in just a moment, as well as the news behind these headlines for those of you who want to get comfortable and learn where this our planet has taken itself today.

(SUPERIMPOSED ON TV SCREEN AS PARROT READS QUICKLY)

ISRAEL, UAR PULL OUT OF DEFEATED TURKEY

Both Sides Deny
Responsibility
of Feeding Turks

US, NATO pullout
Faulted by Ismail;
Yank Aid Demanded

blip

2000 SLAIN IN PANTHER-GYPPIE DEMO

Mayor Arranges
Leader Parley

blip

Thinks Saw Whale
Canada Man Claims

blip

RED TIDE FLOWERS OFF GREECE
US Ag-Aid Department
Denies Any Leak

Fishermen Race
Against Time

blip

Employment in HEW, HUD
Passes That of Industry

blip

Population
of Detroit
Up to 90,000

blip

PIRATES ATTACK WHEAT SHIPMENT

Destroyer Escort Sunk; Israel
AF Rescues; Demands Half Cargo

blip

HEW Chief
Tells Off
President

blip

900 Dead
in Jersey
City Demo

blip

Cloned Colt Still Thrives,
Man Next, Scientist Says

blip

Gyppies Destroy
Two Ohio Towns

blip

Billboard Marks
Wife's Birthday

There it is, ladies and gentlemen, from the ugly to the beautiful, a brief look at today's news in headlines from around the nation and around the world. I'll be back with the story behind every one of those headlines, in just a minute. But now, listen to this, won't you?

Chapter Six

'Mr. Andrews? Chief Kirk in Morehead. We've just got word that a gang pulled a rip on the Rogers place night before last. That's about a mile from you, isn't it?'

'Yeah. You know what happened, Chief?'

Jeff heard Kirk's sigh in his ear, assumed the man was spreading his hands, forgetting that there was no telepickup on the Andrews phone.

'Yeah. The Rogerses are dead, we believe. So are two state troopers who were dumb enough to try to go in to help. Now listen, Mr. Andrews, here's the way it is. There's a hell of a demo raging in Louisville and another in Frankfort. Looks planned, and every Fed's been rushed in there. I've also got a report there's a Gyppie bunch heading this way, out of Ohio.'

'You're telling me not to look for any help,' Jeff said. His eyes met Josie's; she had turned from the sink to stare at him, toweling her hands over and over.

'Ah . . . yeah, Mr. Andrews, that's what I'm telling you.'

'Yeah. Any idea how many there are?'

'No sir. Maybe ten, maybe a few less or a few more. More than five or six, evidently, but we don't *think* there're as many as twenty.'

'How about a copter, Chief?'

'I've got two. One was burned three nights ago. We got 'em, but that doesn't do me any good today. And the mayor has ordered the other one to stay down till we get a definite report on the Gyppies, one way or the other, and then to send it out to check.'

'Yeah. Well, tell the mayor it's a good thing I don't get a chance to vote for him, because one copter could knock out the Rogers place rippers in about seven minutes.'

'Mr. Andrews—'

'Got a family, Chief. Pardon me while I load my guns.' Jeff hung up. He answered the question in Josie's eyes while he dialed Arlie Eldridge.

Then he triggered the alarm, and within three minutes they were all in the living room: Josie and Kristy and Deb, Andy and Scott and Roger, Alex and Jeff. Jeff told them all of it, quietly.

'What about Arlie Eldridge?' Alex asked.

'Arlie got the same call from town. He's getting ready, too. Now look, I'm afraid we're going to have to stop everything and just wait around for them. There's not even a guarantee they'll come here. Kristy goes up to the attic and watches the road. Andy – the other window. Anybody starts through the garden, fire a *rifle* shot, high, and nothing else. NOT the machine gun; let's keep that as a surprise. Maybe a shot will warn 'em off.'

'What if I see somebody down on the road, Daddy?' Kristy asked.

'Well, let's make sure that by somebody you mean a little crowd of people, OK? I mean I don't care if you see a minik or two people walking or something. Take your mother's old bird-watching binocs.'

She nodded. 'Yessir.'

'The rest of us will just check everything out and drop the screens.'

'Dad?' Andy; Jeff looked at him. 'Dad, what if I go up to, say, the Old Fraley Place and keep watch. If I see anyone or hear anyone, I won't do a thing but come back. That way we'll have some advance notice.'

Jeff shook his head. 'We don't need that, Andy, you're just looking for danger. We'll hear shots from Arlie if they come that way.' He grinned. 'OK troops, move out. This is one way to get out of an afternoon's work, anyhow. But let's don't do anything silly. Oh – Kristy, if you and Andy have to pee or anything, do it now, OK? We'll spell you in an hour or two.'

They waited. Kristy came down; Deb and Roger replaced her. Andy came down; Scott went up. The sun wound around to stand above the road, then started slipping rightward. The hill began chewing off its bottom. Deb came down; Josie went up. Andy and Scott changed places again.

At six Jeff telephoned town. Nothing more on the Rogers place rippers, nothing more on the Gyppies. And Mayor Winters' orders about the helicopter stood. Yes, Chief Kirk had told him what Jeff had said. The mayor had merely mentioned that there were less than twenty people out there on that hill, in two houses, and over twenty thousand in Morehead.

At seven they ate, again changing the attic watches. The sun died.

'Reckon 'ere's one vantage livin' in a big city,' Alex said, 'or even near one. TV tells you what's goin' on.'

'Be nice to know, huh?' Jeff shrugged. 'Well, it's beginning to look like night. And I've got an ugly suggestion.'

'I'll go,' Andy said. 'One man'll never be seen, and they aren't about to hear me.'

Jeff looked at him. He shook his head, once. 'Know exactly what I'm going to say, huh? I think we have to, but it won't be you alone. What it should be is you and me, but I hate to pull us both out of here at once.'

'I was thinkin' of me and one of the boys. Andy, probably.'

'Nuh-uh. No trouble for me to say it: be worse if somethin' happent to you'n to me.' He raised a hand, shaking his head. 'Nope, hush. What've I heard you say? You've not gotny false modesty, and dern little of the real kind? OK, don't start changin' now.'

'Alex—'

Alex gazed at him. 'Me an' Andy, Jeff?'

Jeff sat looking at thim. Alex and Andy. Out and through the woods. Along the hillside and down. Along the old fence line and into the orchard, up behind Bill Rogers's place, to see if the rippers were squatting or moving on – or had moved on. In which case they might well be here, and Alex and Andy would be in danger from both sides, even though they would have a tactical advantage: they'd be behind the rippers. But if the rippers were still at the Rogers place, and heard a noise or saw something. . . . Jeff didn't like that one, either. Andy and Alex would most likely not come back. Worse, they might meet the rippers head on, en route. Surprise on both sides – but ten or more rippers wouldn't run from two men. Of course, Alex and Andy should be able to run better, through the dark. But they'd have their backs turned to fusillade after fusillade.

The alternative? Forget it. Stay up all night, waiting. And if they weren't here by morning, wait some more. And on and on – and maybe the rippers would never come, and how long could you remain on – god, he hated the damned military terms – on 'battle alert?'

He nodded. 'Yeah.'

Alex nodded. 'Andy'll be tickled to death.'

'Yeah. ANDY!'

Andy was tickled to death. His pleasure was shared neither by Josie nor by Deb, with both Jeff and Alex trying to act matter-of-fact. So was Andy, but his putting his leg into the wrong leg of his blackpants blew that pose. Scott glowered. Second son, his look said.

They left at a little after nine, taking the submachine gun and the M-20 and pistols, along with the walkie-talkie and one grenade each. Both men were entirely charcoal-dressed – better than black, considerably more shadowy – and gloved and blackfaced. Both Deb and Josie wept, and Jeff sent them both up to the attic, to watch opposite ends. He turned on all the outside lights. Then, after wandering around and around the house for half an hour, he poured himself a long brandy and went into the living room. With the walkie-talkie switched on full volume beside him, he turned on the TV.

He watched the war movie, consciously studying it as a lesson.

General Andrews, he thought, sitting in the goddam war-room watching training films. What in the hell am I doing here? How the hell did it all get this way? Dear god, I'm a *writer.* I'm not a gardener, I hate that kind of work. Farming. Calluses, dirt under the nails, cursing the sun one day and the rain a day or two later and shrieking at the sky if it lets go with a little hail or some snow at the wrong time. And now sitting here with this asinine gun on my hip like some kind of travesty of Wild Bill Hickok, all grim-faced and pretend-confident for the *wimmenfolk,* as if someone were here with cameras shooting another epic of the Old West.

What about cell regeneration and cloning and Mars and Jupiter and Proxima Centauri, what about antigravity and the revolution to turn us into a democracy again, all that stuff I read about and listened to and talked and wrote about? What about all those books and magazines with the yellow hi-liter marks in them, the marginal notes in the fortunately inimitable Andrews chicken scratches, all my notes? Where's the new world that singer said was comin' when I was a kid? What in hell happened to the Age of Aquarius? Where's the mandatory antipregnancy shot I predicted for all girl-kids at about age ten, hating the idea even then because I hate big government? Jesus, three hundred million of us, and the Gyppies are doing everybody a favor, running around killing and destroying.

We've got . . . what, now? About a hundred thousand men in India, pretending there's a UN or ever was, pretending we can do something about the Indians and the Pakistanis killing each other because they're all starving. Another hundred and fifty thousand in Indochina, playing peace-keepers, with the President and Congress probably hoping somebody will jump all over 'em, drop a nuke on 'em, so we can get into one hell of a war and drain off all this excess population, all this damned human meat. And me sittin' here hoping they don't, because then Andy would probably lose his deferment as a non-city dweller, and in less than a year, if that kind of war lasted that long, Scott would lose his, too. And somebody's rip us off with them gone because Alex and I are coming on for forty-five and then fifty, and our reflexes just naturally aren't as good.

What? Thirty thousand men in Italy? About that, although we're told there are twenty thousand. Supposedly keeping Vatican City safe (for what? Democracy? Shit! Democracy's one thing *il Papa's* got no time for!). No, we've got all those troops over there to make damned certain he doesn't forget he and his council of ancients have a time-limit on how long they can dilly-dally before they draft that Bull on family control.

So what if he doesn't? We going to declare war on Vatican City and then Italy, and wind up fighting Spain too and exempting all Catholics from service? *Sure* we are; that would take the same kind of guts it would have taken in the sixties to call off Indochina and start cramming all that money into Ecology, Doing Something About Destruction Of.

TICK!

Jeff jerked. Alex had snapped his finger against his w-t speaker. He and Andy were in the orchard behind the Rogers house. He waited; no, just one snick. The house was still there, then.

His heart started machine-gunning, spurting blood in all directions through him, making him gasp for breath and start Yogic deep breathing to keep the silly pump from banging right through his chest.

Field reports back to HQ: destination reached. Jesus Christ, what a lot of . . . oh dear god, why can't a man just write, speak, raise hell and drink and screw his wife and watch what his kids become? Why the screw does he have to play farmer to stay alive, play general to stay alive, sit around here waiting for the sound of gunfire on the w-t or a sqawk from the attic?

TICK TICK!

There were people at the Rogers place. The rippers, or at least some of them, were still there.

Why aren't we cloning people, using the ability to change the sex of unborn kids to stop hemophilia and even color-blindness? Why aren't we regenerating lost parts, creating geniuses with cloning and RNA? Why the hell does a nation get to the point where it has to outlaw public attendance at athletic events because you just can't let all those rats get together in one cage? Why can't kids go to college and make eyes at each other and have dates and neck and play mutual mastur and shackup? How can TV replace the social contact of a bunch of kids swarming all over a pretty campus, growing up in mind and body and figuring out who's going to date and lay who and who is maybe a for-keeps partner, and arguing about Sartre and Rand and Gibran. Who made us close the colleges?

The kids? The pro demo-organizers? The National Guard? The President who signed the bill, poor bastard? Shit no. All his cowardly asinine politicking predecessors, who took industry's money and couldn't tell them to stop poisoning everybody, who traded cars every two years just like everybody else because it was status and besides the cars were programmed to fall apart the third year anyhow, all the bastards who were afraid to offend the Catholics and the hardshell Baptists and whatever else by making some loud noises about birth control. God, there was a time when they'd have offended *me*, because Josie and I were born that way and were Catholic almost thirty years. Blame the Catholics? Lord no; all our friends were sure as hell ready for a little rule-changing when we were all breeding like hawgs, but we didn't stand up and scream about that anymore than we screamed about oil on the beaches or the Red Tides killing fish and people too, or all the other things we should have been cracking heads over.

If Azodrin doesn't succeed in ridding your cotton of all those nasty insects, fellers, why, that means there are more pesky bugs coming in from someplace else, not that they're grooving on the stuff. Just lay more Azodrin on 'em, fellers, us folks at Shell Chemical know what's good for you, and who needs a few hundred thousand birds more or less, anyhow?

Drink your milk, honey, Strontium 90's GOOD for you.

Eat your apples, kids, an apple a day keeps the doctor away, and man that DDT's just naturally great stuff.

Use all the paper you can, dears, it's good for the economy, and trees grow fast.

Pregnant? Well, you'll have to get married, then, honey, because you've been wicked and you have to be punished, man has to pay for his pleasures, and so what for the rest of your life, damn you, mommy TOLD you not to screw! ABORTION! Oh god, I have raised a murderous monster who is not only a little whore but would slay a poor unborn fetus out of hand rather than allow it to grow and bloat her and be born to help fill up the cage.

Kids have a RIGHT to be born; we're going to be the biggest country ever was, and besides the government may need that kid in Indochina or someplace.

Gonna be no population problem, folks, why this country's got millions and millions of acres in national parks, and we could build houses and apartments and roads for good ole automobiles on them for the next hunnert years and *still* never run out of trees and *lebensraum.* But get those damned redwoods out of the way, they're too big and take up too much room and boy can you get a lot of wood out of one of them for more good old lecterns for politicians to stand behind and holler about pollution and ecology!

What we need is another bubonic plague, Jeff Andrews thought, to weed us out again. But if that happened . . . what the hell guarantee do I have that it won't come right up on this hill and weed us out along with the rest? That kind of thing gets pretty damned personal!

(Who was the greatest man ever? Cain; he killed a quarter of the world's population!)

What we need is to forget everything we ever learned about chemistry, and to know as much about botany as we do physics.

Yes, he thought, wouldn't that have been nice . . . no penicillin (oops; did that derive from botany?) . . . no DDT, no . . .

Dream fictions. Shut it off. Nonsense. Physics and chemistry are more spectacular, and people just naturally like to see kids born and to see how long they can live, and the two desires are perhaps not quite but certainly damnear mutually incompatible!

(Cain, Cain: Where are you now that we need you?)

'Alex,' the walkie-talkie said quietly beside him, and Jeff jerked. 'What if I move up and leave the w-t by the house and then we get on out of here? About twelve people in there, Jeff, both sexes. Partying, drunk I think, or high on something. Not Gyppies. Hell, we c'd use both grenades and that'd be it, right now.'

Jeff tapped the speaker with his nail in acknowledgment and in hopes Alex would turn his receiving volume down, way down.

'What about the Rogerses?'

'No sign. But the house's been shot up, and we *think* we'n see blood inside; hard to tell from here, even with the glasses.'

'Want to blow them up if they aren't all dead?'

'No, but if there are any Rogerses alive, Jeff, there sure won't be any when these people leave.'

Damn! He could say yeah, lob in the grenades, and he and his hill and his family would be safe – this time. And he'd always wonder what if he hadn't. Or they could just leave the rippers there. Maybe they were squatters and that would be that, they'd have to be accepted if they worked the land. Or the troubles in Louisville and Frankfort would work themselves out and there'd be Feps over here, or the Gyppies would be heading somewhere else and the Morehead chopper could come out and take care of the menace to Jeff's hill.

'Got another suggestion,' he said. 'Not too pleasant.'

'You want us to go in?'

'God no! No, I mean get way the hell back in the orchard and stay there, see what they do, fade out if they start leaving.'

'Don't bother me none,' Alex muttered. 'Andy?'

'Few chiggers never killed anybody,' Andy said quietly.

'We'll stay then,' Alex said.

'Alex, Andy? Just get way back, and for god's sake don't do anything silly, OK? Stay out of sight.'

'Outta sight,' Andy said.

'I'm going to bed. I'll take the w-t with me. We've all got to get rested.' He didn't bother saying it; he knew Alex and Andy would spell each other sleeping, or trying to sleep.

He told the others in the house, went over it again, assuring a lip-biting Josie and a tear-leaking Deb that the two men were in no more danger than anyone in the house. Then he went upstairs with the walkie-talkie and held Josie until they both went to sleep and he woke up with an arm gone to sleep and a cramped leg and loud voices in his ears, strange voices.

Chapter Seven

'Why can't we just stay here, Ray? I mean gosh, a whole house, and all these apples and things. . . .'

'It's an invitation, Elly. A damned open invitation, that's all. Look how easy it was for us to take it over!'

'Besides, there isn't room for all of us to live here,' a third voice said. 'We'd be at each other's throats in days.'

'Russ?' A fourth voice, coming in loud and clear from the walkie-talkie beside Jeff's bed. He avoided Josie's wide eyes. They were hearing all these strangers over the w-t. . . . *where were Andy and Alex?*

'Russ? What if we split up, some of us stayed here to hold this place, homestead? All those apples – we could sell them for plenty, in a month or whenever it is they get big enough to fall off the trees.'

'Jesus Christ, asshole, you wanna be a sinkin' dirt-farmer? So stay here with your damned apples then, and lotsa luck! Not me, boy, I'm gonna see who else lives around here, and what they've got to offer, like a little meat or booze.'

'And mostly daughters,' a sixth voice said, with a laugh in it, and Jeff felt sick. He forwned; that sounded like a girl, whimpering.

'Listen, what makes those lacy things in the trees like that?' the voice called Elly asked.

'Caterpiggles,' another girl told her.

'Hey . . . look, that's a walkie-talkie hangin' up there! Like somebody just left it there.'

'Be damned, Russ, yer right! Why would they do that?'

'The people in the house,' someone suggested. 'Maybe they put it there to hear us if we'd come in this way.'

'Hey, yeah.'

'Good thing we came in the other way!'

'Listen, these hillbillies got all sorts of tricks. Remember that beartrap?'

'Who the hell could forget? It damnear got me!'

Laughing: 'I'll say they know all kinds of tricks! That girl was about the best sink I've had since that place last month, where they had the twins.'

Jeff closed his eyes. Bill Rogers' daughter Ann. . . .

'Betcha can't knock that thing out of the tree in one shot.'

'Bet the hell I can!'

'Wait a minute – how about if we climbed up and got it?'

'What the hell use is one walkie-talkie, asshole?'

'Maybe the other one's in the house?' Elly's voice. High, young. All of them sounded young.

'Didn't see it.'

Russ: 'We'd have seen it. It would have been hanging up in the bedroom or someplace like that, where they'd hear anybody out here. Naw . . . I wonder why?'

'Maybe – hey, Russ, maybe—' the voice lowered—' 'maybe somebody's listening to us right now.'

Silence. Then Russ's voice, followed by a chorus: 'SINK YOU!'

And then BANG, a rifle, and another bang, and that was that; they'd got the w-t with the second shot.

'Jeff?' Josie touched his shoulder. 'Jeff? Andy. . . .'

'It's OK, sweetheart,' he said, turning the w-t off and turning to grip her shoulder and squeeze; she loved strength. 'They hung the thing up in a tree for just this, so we could hear the rippers. They're on their way back right now.'

'Are you sure?'

He touched her lips with his; she clung. 'Sure,' he said. What else was there for a man to say? 'Let's get some breakfast ready; they'll be along pretty soon.'

'What time is it?'

He checked. 'Seven,' he said, and suddenly he was remembering how he'd always got up at eight-thirty or nine, because he preferred staying up late to rising early. Seven o'clock. He was a farmer now; no, a half-ass farmer, because a farmer worth his equipment depreciation allowance was up at 4:30 or 5.

Andy and Alex were in the kitchen, drinking coffee.

'Why the hell didn't you keep the thing and ease back, with one eye on them,' Jeff demanded after Josie had embarrassed her son by hugging him hard and tight and Jeff had grinned at them both, squeezing their arms in delight at seeing them.

'Because they started yelling, 'bout midnight,' Alex said. 'Told somebody named Jim to get out in the orchard and keep watch, with Gary. Tiger here,' Alex nudged Andy with his elbow, 'wanted to grab Jim and Gary, like commandoes, and bring 'em back. One peep and we'd have been mobbed, so we vamoosed. I was up in the tree with the walkie-talkie, and I had this idea to turn it on full and just leave it.'

'OK,' Jeff said, 'I'm sorry. Well, they're all out there now, or seven or eight of them anyhow, with two girls, and I thought I heard another one, whimpering. Talking about what a good lay Ann Rogers was, and how much fun this was, and maybe they should stay and harvest the apples – they think you wait for them to fall off the trees – and so on. Guy named Russ is in charge. They all sound young. City. He wants to move on – he sounds like a professional wanderer, ripper, murderer.'

Alex and Andy nodded in silence. Their eyes showed they were thinking about Ann Rogers and her mother.

'Then they shot the w-t,' Jeff said.

'Shit!' Alex pounded his thigh with his fist. 'I'da thoughta that, I'd notta left it.'

'Yeah well, we're short a w-t and . . . some neighbors. And we're probably target one, unless Arlie – oh.'

Jeff telephoned Arlie, gave him the story. Then he called the police number in town. The copter wasn't there; there were about forty Gyppies raising hell all around Olive Hill, and the copter and thirty Morehead policemen, in three cars, had gone over there.

They awoke the others and reposted the attic window sentinels. Within an hour Deb tripped the alarm. They all rushed upstairs to watch the activity down on the highway: Three vehicles, and there was no mistaking the rippers. The third machine was Bill Rogers' old armored pickup truck.

Jeff called Arlie Eldridge again.

About two minutes later Arlie called back. The bunch was coming up the hill, passing his road because his house was invisible through the trees. They were following the curving road toward Jeff's – and they were there before he hung up.

They drew up on the road above the house, just in the flat after the curve where the garage used to be. Two rechargeable-battery electricars and the Rogers pickup truck. House and vehicles watched each other.

Then Jeff, carrying his rifle at trail and wearing his holstered revolver, went out the back door. He walked the few steps to the big old silver maple and stood there, half behind it, gazing at the three vehicles across the yard and up the terrace, something like a hundred feet away. He wore his miner's helmet.

(Hardhat. Why/when had helmets become hardhats? Because 'helmet' sounded military/militant, and people always seemed to think that roses by another name had less thorns?)

'Hey there,' a voice called. Jeff recognized it, although he'd heard it only over the w-t. But it had been a good one, without much tinny distortion. This was the leader Russ.

'Hey yourself.'

The door of the first car opened. A young man or boy got out. Short-haired, city style. Mustached. Red-blonde hair, no sideburns, pale eyes, a chin that could have been stronger or used a beard. He wore a dark figured shirt outside his jeans. And a holstered revolver, low on his thigh on a big black belt.

Bet he watches the TV religiously, Jeff mused, *and practices and* practices *his fast-draw! Got the hip-swagger down pretty good; what's it to him those guys in the Western movies walk that way because of their high-heeled boots? If baseball players were the big rage now, everybody like this creature would walk with that odd flat-footed gait a man has to adopt when he wears a shoe full of spikes.*

'Uh – we're lost,' the boy said. Russ.

'Um.' Jeff nodded. 'No wonder, if you start turnin' off on every dirt road you pass. Saw you go by on the highway a few minutes ago. If you'd kept on straight, you'd have come to the pike. U.S. 60.'

'Oh. Thanks. Uh – could we have a drink, Mister? A little water?'

'You travel without water?'

'Ran out,' Russ said, smiling easily.

'I'm sorry,' Jeff said, watching two others, both male, get out of the second car, the white one. They looked young, mean. Not tough; mean. 'You know how it is with us hillsiders, and we haven't had much rain for a while.' He pretended to relent. 'Aww – tell you what. Let two of your people come on down to the house, with containers, and you can fill 'em up from the hose.' He gestured at the spigot and coiled hose a few yards behind him, at the corner of the house.

'Umm . . . two of my people? My people? Mister, we aren't a gang or anything like that. We're just—' he waved his arms – young people, trying to get to . . . Knoxville.'

Sure you are, Jeff thought. *And Ann Rogers is alive and well and* puella integra, *too, you swaggering murderer.*

He shrugged. 'Well . . . we've learned to be a little

cautious.' He smiled. 'You know how it is, young feller.' *Sound like you were born to work the land, Andrews,* he told himself, *sound like your daddy and your daddy's daddy were farmers, dropping out of school as soon as they reached sixteen and even earlier when they could. Teach him contempt. No, pander to it; this fart's contemptuous of everyone and everything; he thinks youth and reflexes are all there are in the world, and he's got both, and everyone else is stupid and deserving of death. And he's the Hand of God.*

Nodding, Russ was looking around. 'Sure is a pretty place, Mister. Garden up there, all these nice trees – my folks sure would love it. Wouldn't believe it. I don't believe either one of them's been out of North Philly in their lives. You work it alone?'

'Naw,' Jeff said, noting that he was now covered by two rifles laid along the hoods of the cars. 'My wife helps. Boys went off to the city, couple of years ago.' He flicked a sweat-bee off his forearm.

Russ gazed at him, standing loose, hand away from his holster and the protruding gunbutt. 'You mean there's just the two of you up here? With all that house and all this space?'

'Yeah,' Jeff said, 'I reckon so.'

Russ laughed. 'Well, Mister, I think this's too much space for just you two. There's a lot more of us than you, and we need all this space a lot worse. We're younger, the future of the world.'

God forbid, Jeff thought.

'So why don't you just call your wife on out here, Mister.'

'Don't reckon I ought to do that,' Jeff said.

'Mister, you've got two rifles aimed right at your gut. Now you just turn around and call your wife. What's the dear lady's name?'

'Alex,' Jeff said, and Russ's laughter was echoed by several of his companions. Jeff turned toward the house, bending his knees a little.

'Alex,' he called. 'OPEN UP!' And Jeff flexed his knees

and was behind the maple, his back to Russ and his people. He hoped the maple was big enough. The best defense, he'd told Alex, was one hell of a strong offensive, and Alex had nodded in silence.

Alex opened up. As they'd agreed, he used only the rifle, but Alex with a rifle was as good as anyone else with a submachine gun.

Crack, and crack again, and crack a third time, and yelling and screaming and doors slamming and engines gunning and the big engine of the Rogers pickup roaring and gravel and dirt flying. Jeff edged leftward, around the tree a little as the three cars ran the gauntlet, racing down the road past the house and around the curve and up and away, around the hill where the garden was. Jeff peered out, saw the tail end of the truck vanishing.

Jeff ran.

He sprinted across the yard, rushed up the terrace and across the road and up the knoll, trying to make time without trampling anything in the garden. But his charge up that knoll was unnecessary; the three vehicles were rushing back down the hill the way they'd come, hardly slowing down for that first right-angle turn. He stood there and watched them disappear. He was breathing hard.

When he turned, Josie was there. She held him close, trying to burrow her head in through his chest.

'You weren't supposed to leave the house, dammit!'

She clung the tighter. 'Your wife came out, mister,' she said against his chest, and he splayed his hand across her back, then squeezed. He glanced back. The three ripper vehicles were gone, nearly out of earshot as well as sight. With an arm – his left – around Josie, Jeff returned to their road.

Alex's first shot, a complete surprise, had been too valuable to waste on Russ. Two of Russ' band had been behind the cars, each with a rifle trained on Jeff. Alex had shot the first one, shearing away the top of his head – it was on the edge of the road, several feet behind the body. Then Alex, cool and imperturbable, too sure of himself to bother checking that target, had twitched his barrel a little to the right and squeezed again, and put a bullet into the other rifleman's face between his upper lip and his nose. The third shot had been aimed at Russ, but had missed as Russ had turned and dived. The shots Jeff had hardly been aware of, nine or ten of them, had starred a windshield, shattered a back window and driven on into a cheek or neck, and ricocheted off various plates of armor. Russ had hurled himself into the back of the pickup truck and Alex had spent three bullets trying to hit him. He was certain he had not, and he was apologetic about the bullets.

'One thing about them fellers,' he said grinning. 'They sure do think you've got a sharpshootin' wife, Mister.'

Jeff shook his head, noting that his hands were trembling as he rolled a cigaret. 'You are a bloodthirsty monster, Alex.'

Alex nodded solemnly. Deb's eyes seemed to flash and her mouth came open angrily, to remind Jeff of the Rogerses. But she saw her husband's face, looked at Jeff's. He gave her a quiet smile. She sighed, telling them silently that once again she had failed to appreciate the strange sense of humor of the two men.

Andy put down the phone, frowning.

'Dad? Arlie says they passed his place as if they had wolves under their tails, and Mister Pennington says they haven't come down the road, and the Hargises haven't seen them either.'

And there'd been no cry from Kristy at the attic window upstairs.

Jeff and Alex looked at each other. 'Damn. They've stopped down where the old school was, to lick their wounds.'

Alex nodded. 'They'll be back.'

MEANWHILE: IV

A City Is a Ghastly Place to Live, But What Choice Does Helen Caudill Have?

Helen Caudill's notes toward an essay, *Seeking A Better World.*

'COME, MY FRIENDS, 'TIS NOT TOO LATE TO BUILD A BETTER WORLD.'

—Alfred, First Baron Tennyson, about 1850

[Tennyson was educated by his father at home, except for four years at grammar school, much like now. In 1839 T. carried funds to the Pyrenees through France, for the Spanish anti-monarchists. I can find that he did nothing else other than write poetry, although his play *The Promise of May* was an attack on the rationalist movement in England. Maybe he thought that was building a better world.]

1967: the U.S. government allocated 28 billion dollars to the solution of "urban problems". Robert Weaver, Secretary of Housing and Urban Development, performed the annual rite of begging Congress for more money.

[Compare T. and Weaver; both said nice things, but neither DID anything. T. was one of 11 children; find out how many *he* had.]

'We are seeing more and more non-infectious respiratory disease in children.' Doctor Marquis, in W. Virginia, c. 1970.

At the time, Charleston, W. Va., was called the Chemical Center of the World. It was also called Death Valley.

Allen Taylor, Ph.D. (Chemistry), accepting Ehrlich Award for Ecological Furthering: 'They won't listen to us, gentlemen, not to you and me. We are scientists, and we can talk all day and all night, but they look upon us as part of the *cause* of the problem. We aren't *medical* scientists, you see. We just aren't considered competent witnesses to prove cause and effect ratios, and people only half-trust us anyhow, including judges. What we need is to get every physician, every medical researcher and practicing M.D. in the country into court. That's what we need, if we are to save ourselves. But can you think of a busier group of people? Can you think of any class of people that is more overworked in these perilous times? *No* group of people in the world has *less* time to spare for appearing in court, waiting around for the whim of gravelly old judges. And who can convince Mrs. McGillicuddy that the reason her doctor isn't in this morning to patch up junior's knee – or let us be serious, to treat Junior's strange and apparently non-infectious respiratory disease – is that Doctor is in court, trying to save millions of juniors all over the country and the world, all with one testimony? I say to you gentlemen that we must *subpoena* the doctors!'

Rene Dubos ['60's]: 'Man has a remarkable ability to develop some form of tolerance to conditions extremely different from those under which he evolved.' [but he *can't* be expected to adapt to] '. . . insults with which he has had no experience in his evolutionary past. . . .'

'Walter Reuther and Henry Ford poisoned the American people as surely as had they been named Borgia, and now their successors are doing so on an even greater scale – and they KNOW the problem!' – Clarke Fannin, *Los Angeles Free Press*, 1974. [Sued for libel or slander; *check which is which.*]

'We is met the enemy and he is us.' – Pogo [check to find out who Pogo was.] [Find out who wrote 'Make Room, Make Room!']

COME, MY FRIENDS, 'TIS NOT TOO LATE TO BUILD A BETTER WORLD.

[Isn't it?]

Chapter Eight

Alex was right. The rippers came back. But it wasn't a rip-off, or even an attack. It was a massacre.

The house was dark. The outside spotlights were off. Jeff and Alex were in the attic, with Deb and Kristy; the attic windows, nearly thirty feet above the ground, commanded excellent views on both sides of the house. The others waited in the darkened house downstairs, all armed and ready behind double-barred doors and the iron window screens.

There was more tension in the house, Scott had said, than there was in the power lines. His father had remarked the remark. It was the kind of thing that came from minds that were trying to be writers, and once Scot got all that old Poe-type imagery out of his head he might be the writer in the family yet.

Of course it's true, Jeff thought, squeezing his eyes shut after too much staring out at nothing. We just can't accept that sort of poetry in writing anymore. It wasn't Stein or Hemingway who recycled it, it was reality. It made people take all the purtiness out of things, including literature, and made articles more popular than short stories, destroying magazines fist over hand. I'll bet—

But he had opened his eyes, and looked out, and he'd seen something. He was at the northwest window, the one that looked down the long steep hill to the big road. The road was plainly marked by its luminous center- and side-stripes. What he had seen was a damsight closer, just over the hill, just below the cesspool. He squinted. The peach-tree trembled, and he swept his gaze back and forth, but nothing else was moving. There was no breeze.

Then he heard the sound of a throat's being cleared, and a moment later moonlight glinted on metal: a gun barrel.

The damned fools had ignored the tree cover and gone to all the trouble to climb this dear hillside.

Extending his right hand behind him, he snapped his fingers. That was enough; Alex snapped his in return. Silently, Kristy slipped downstairs and Deb crept over to Jeff's side.

Kristy would tell the others the location of the rippers, and would incidentally be out of the way of (A) the horrible things Jeff did not want her to see, and (B) return fire.

Deb slipped the bottle into his hand. Alex was creeping over from the other side of the attic.

'Don't see nothin',' he whispered. Alex *really* whispered; his voice carried no more than four or five feet when he spoke in normal tones. 'Gwon over 'ere and watch, Deb. I'm better here.'

She touched his arm, then crawled across the attic.

Jeff could see Alex in the paleness of his face. 'Ready?'

The paleness moved; Alex was nodding. Jeff took a deep breath.

Then he struck a match, applied it to the cloth he'd forced into the top of the bottle, and tossed it out the window. It swung out and up a little, flashing in the moonlight like a diminutive, fire-trailing rocket. It dropped, and someone yelled, and then the bottle struck and exploded and fire leaped into the air in liquid splashes. Even amid the shrieks and yells, Jeff thought: *shame to destroy that peach tree.*

But there were screams and shouts and bellows and high keening shrieks from the hillside below, and shots, and he and Alex squatted on either side of the window and pumped shot after shot out into the night.

A figure from a horror movie sprang from the flames and started running down the hill, screaming like a wounded horse, waving its fiery arms and trailing flames like a billowing yellow-orange cloak. Jeff ceased his indiscriminate fire long enough to put two into the poor man's back, then lowered his muzzle and fired again into the flaming horseweeds and peach tree and forsythia on the hillside.

Alex grunted, set aside his rifle, and suddenly the submachine gun was stuttering, sounding like the much magnified backspace key on Jeff's electric typewriter.

The flames went on and on; the screams went on and on. There were fewer shouts and shots from below. Someone in a white shirt was pellmelling down the hill, staying on his feet for no reason other than his momentum, and Jeff raised his rifle again. Nothing happened; it was empty. By the time he had thrust it at Deb, Alex had already sprayed the running ripper. The arms stopped windmilling, but the legs kept on running for several more steps until it fell.

The noise was awful, deafening, screams shots yells crackling fire tommygun stutter, and Jeff wished he'd had sense enough to take time out to put in his earplugs before he'd thrown the molotov to light up the hillside and confuse the enemy. He winced, opened his mouth wide and blinked. He continued firing.

Someone came up over the edge of the hill, ran smack into the white ash, fell and rolled and crawled. Jeff tried to swing his rifle, but Alex was in the way – Jeff was in Alex's way – and the ripper was out of sight, in the yard behind the house.

Jeff swung around. 'ONE'S IN THE BACKYARD! THE BACKYARD!' He could barely hear his own shout above the babababa noise of the submachine gun, but he knew the shout would separate itself out to those downstairs. Which scared him, and he wished he hadn't shouted. Suppose Andy or Josie ran out there and—

Alex ran out of ammunition.

The almost-silence was strange, a new world, as if they had been submerged in an unplumbed ocean of ear-ripping sound for ages, the way it had been in the old SST days, before the screams of the people had grown even louder than the booms of the aircraft and Nixon's Folly had been outlawed.

(Shame he had to be remembered that way; he'd ended the Vietnam thing, as nearly as it could be ended, but everyone remembered him chiefly for Black Friday and the supersonic transport fiasco.)

Flames crackled, and there were moans. And not another sound, save for the panting, which Jeff realized after a while was his. He should have known; insouciant Alex probably hadn't raised his temperature or blood pressure a hundredth of a point.

'Hang right here,' Jeff said, and he nearly bowled Deb over as he ran crouching to the steps and rushed down them to bounce off the door at the bottom, swing around through the bedroom and the hall and down the steps again. The back hall light was on.

'Andy!'

'Jeff! Andy went out the back door!' Josie's voice, screaming, terrified, Jeff ran. She jerked aside as he went through the kitchen and out the open door and into the yard. Switching his rifle to his left hand, he drew his pistol with his right.

Two figures – nonsense; two human beings – were wrestling in the moonlit backyard. Jeff rushed to them, saw that Andy was on top and apparently in control. He dropped to one knee beside them, reholstering the pistol and leveling his rifle at the edge of the hill, covering them.

No one else came up over the hill. And there were no more shots. And no more screams, no more shouts. Some moans, the grunts of the two people beside him, the crackle of the flames.

'Knee him in the balls or smash his throat, Andy, and come on,' Jeff snapped, without glancing at them. 'We've got to get that fire out, now.'

'Da-ad,' Andy grunted, gasping, 'dammit – it isn't a – he!'

Jeff swung, thrust the barrel of his rifle in past Andy's arm, and snuggled it up against a white cheek.

'Relax, girl, or I'll blow your little head off.'

She made a noise like a squeak and was limp. Andy swung off her, carefully. Her clothes were torn. Andy picked up his pistol.

Jeff was watching the hill's edge again. 'Are you hurt?'

'No sir.'

'Not you, dammit. Are you hurt, girl?'

No reply. Andy bent over her. 'She's unconscious. Fainted, I imagine. I don't think she's hurt. She could sure run, and fight, too!'

'All right, dumb-ass, pick her up and get her in the house, then. If you'd *used* that damned gun instead of playing Galahad we wouldn't have to worry about her. Take her in and tell Josie to tie 'er up. And come straight back.'

Andy carried the girl in without a word. Jeff duck-walked over to the white ash, rifle hip-held and finger curled within the guard. But there was no one. Only the smell. Fire, gasoline, and – roast flesh.

When he peered around the slender tree he saw the white, white hand; just over the lip of the hill and clutching. But it didn't move. Whoever belong to it was out of the fight. And Alex was already blazing away from the attic window – but this time he was using the hose that ran down to the tap in the upstairs bathroom. The fire hissed angrily. Then Andy was back, with the extinguisher, and he held the rifle while Jeff, still crouching, sent its smothering stream out over the hillside.

The gasoline had already burned itself out. The peach tree was gone, along with the forsythia and horse weeds that had been caught in the explosion and the intensity of that first roaring sheet of tongue-hurling flame. But the vegetation was green, and there were no trees, and the fire was easy to control, then kill.

Andy and Jeff waited, crouching side by side. They heard no sound, either of movement or human voice.

'They must all be dead or escaped,' Andy muttered.

'I don't think any escaped,' Jeff told him quietly, and felt his son tremble beside him. He knew that he would, too, later. But not until he was in bed and enwrapped in Josie's arms, with her held close in his.

'We – we'd better check, Dad. Someone might be wounded, and passed out.'

'Accept this, son. If that's so, it isn't worth the risk, and it's HOT down there. If someone's hurt and unconscious, he'll just have to do without the luxury of treatment until morning.'

'Dad!'

'Yeah.'

Silence. Then, 'You're right. How can a man make himself so rational, when emotion says go do something.'

'Read my book about Genghis Khan again, son, then study our actions in and after Korea and Nam. And read that fem-lib stuff, that business about men's being stupid, and fighting war with rules. Rules and emotion kill, son, but they don't kill the enemy,' Jeff said, and it sounded pat and sententious to him, and he sighed and shut up.

They went back into the house. Josie grabbed them both, shivering and muttering things the fem-libs had never thought of. Josie was a woman.

So was the prisoner. No, not a woman, a dirty-faced, dirty-clothed girl, maybe Andy's age and maybe a year or two older or younger. City-short brown hair so dark it was almost black. Full lips and odd eyelashes – oh, they were mostly gone, and her brows were crisped and curled. She wasn't burned; radiant heat had frizzed her short hair and pretty much relieved her of brows and lashes. Her blouse was torn, and one of those super-tight city bras showed through, with pale flesh half-mooning softly above it. A city girl, yes; they wore loose blouses and tight brassieres and short hair, trying to appear as sexless as possible. Everybody was a target in the jungle existence of cities, but the sexier a girl looked the more risks and trouble rippers and muggers and all the other animals would accept to get her.

She was thin. City-thin.

Jeff wondered. Was this one of the voices on the walkie-talkie? Elly, who'd wanted someone named Ray to remain and homestead the bullet-riddled and doubtless blood-spattered and -smelling house they'd ripped off? The other one, the one who'd said 'caterpiggles?' Or the one he'd thought he had heard, whimpering? And why those bruises on her face and arm? They weren't put there tonight, they were purpling, old.

Then, because he could not keep his eyes from the rent in her blouse, he saw the other bruise. With a little black line in its center. A cut, in her left breast. Days old.

'Josie? Josie . . . untie her, and you and Andy take her upstairs. Andy: you come back. Josie – honey, strip her and put her in a warm tub, will you?'

She was staring at him, frowning a little.

'She's filthy,' he said, in what he knew was a defensive manner. 'Don't leave her, sweetheart, just sit right there on the toilet and watch her. Give her a robe, nothing else, when she's through in the tub.' He edged closer to his wife. 'Those bruises aren't new,' he muttered.

Josie nodded. She untied the unconscious girl, and she and Andy took her upstairs. Andy came back down with a faraway look on his face.

'Dad. . . .'

'Don't ask me yet, son. We'll have to wait till she's conscious and clean and we can talk to her. And after that – I *still* don't know what the hell we do with a ripper prisoner. I sure wish you'd shot her.'

Andy stood gazing at him. He didn't say anything. From the basement came the sound of the overworked water pump; from upstairs came the sound of water rushing into the bathtub.

Second verse
Same as the first
A little bit louder
And a little bit worse. . . .

—refrain learned at a Christian Youth
Fellowship conclave, c. 1950

MEANWHILE: V

A City Is a Helluva Place to Live, But It's a Place to Live

The armored truck pulled slowly away from the light and crawled along with the traffic flow until it reached the corner of High and Woodland, where the church had been before they burned it. The armored truck turned down Woodland, tooled along beneath the dying old trees. The driver sat easily, calmly, his eyes straight ahead, shifting now and again to the rearview mirror. Beside him, Shotgun sat less relaxedly, his eyes ever amove, seeking, seeking that which he hoped he never saw. His hands were sweaty around the shotgun. He was thirty-five, and it wasn't a bad job, so long as you never had to use the scatter-gun. He never had, and he'd had this job for seven years. But he had a buddy who'd been killed, just a year ago, when they'd rolled a bottle full of gasoline and old rag and fire under his armored car and then shot both him and the driver when they came out.

A car approached them from the opposite direction, and Shotgun's hands tensed until it was past and the driver grunted as his eyes followed it in the rearview; it was OK, it was going on. Shotgun watched the little band of six youths, four blacks and two whites, as they swaggered along the sidewalk. They looked back at him, and one of them gave him the finger, then two others. Bastards! That kind he almost wished would try something. Pumping a load of buckshot right into their goddam snotty sneering faces would be a pleasure.

They crossed Maxwell, passed a man and a woman walking together. Shotgun thought: *Snap it up, folks. Six of the toughest coming along behind you!*

On the other hand, he thought, it would be two less mouths to feed, and besides the woman had a good tail and he wouldn't mind a little of that himself.

The street was quiet and deserted, close-crowded old houses staring back at them blank-eyed, iron screens lowered. One of them sported what looked like a pair of bullet holes in the doorjamb. They stopped in front of the house two doors down. What a waste, Shotgun thought. All these houses. And so strange; just across the street was a block-long hiRise accommodating far more people on one floor than all these little houses did, put together. Why the hell didn't those bastards down at cityhall do something about this sort of thing? People sleeping in the streets, newlyweds living with mom and dad until a new apartment building was completed, and all these scummy people living here this way, with a half a house per family . . . and in some cases, even a whole house!

The car behind them passed, and the driver pulled across the street and into the driveway beside the hiRise. There was a big brick wall, and the three filthy kids sitting on it thumbed noses or hoisted middle fingers as the armored car passed. Their mouths moved, too, but of course neither the driver nor Shotgun could hear them.

Two respirator-masked guys were waiting near the back doors, but when Shotgun raised his weapon so they could see it, they frowned and backed off. The driver pulled up until the front bumper – two inches thick and three feet high – was almost touching the big door. He plucked the com off the dashboard, identified himself, gave the codeword. The door rose and the armored car drove in to the ground-level parking basement of the hiRise. He eased his truck right over to the elevator.

Shotgun got out, looked around, and went to the com beside the elevator. He knew the numbers, and he punched them.

'Caudill.'

'Miz Caudill?'

'This is her daughter Helen. Who is that?'

'Kroger,' he said, and gave the numbers and the daycode.

'Oh good – we'll be right down!'

Shotgun nodded at the driver, backed off to lean against

a cement wall, his eyes roving. He waited, checking his watch. A minute and a half passed before the elevator light flashed and the thing said 'ding.' He swung his shotgun toward it, waiting as the doors wheezed back. A boy and a girl came out. They looked at the truck, then automatically glanced right, knowing where Shotgun would be.

'Ross Caudill, junior,' the boy said; he looked about eighteen.

'Helen Caudill,' the girl said. She appeared about the same age, and she wasn't a bad-looking one, either. One nice thing about this job riding shotgun, even with the danger. You got to see a lot of sinkbait in their inside clothes. This one, for instance, popped his eyes in a shirt that had creased and lines running back from her breasts, and a skirt that was no more than knee-length. And she was barefoot.

The boy gave him their numbers, and Shotgun checked them against the delivery receipt. He nodded, gave them his ID and the daycode again. Then he signaled the driver, who spoke into his com, so that when Shotgun opened up the truck's back door the inner lock was also released and the guard inside grinned and lowered his gun. Shotgun stepped back, glancing around.

Ross and Helen Caudill unloaded their three bags of groceries, thanked the delivery men, and went back into the elevator. The delivery truck was already backing around to leave when the elevator doors closed.

Chapter Nine

'. . . and little Israel, the most productive nation in the world in comparison to its size and population, continues to beat off a hungry Mediterranean Alliance. After today's raid on the Israeli industrial center of Amman in which seventeen Greek aircraft were shot down. Greek premier Vasilu Varsakelis said that people in his country are, quote, being forced to cannibalism, end quote. President Isaacson of Israel pooh-poohed the statement, but added that even if such an incredible monstrosity could be true, Israel had no food to spare for its friends, much less its self-avowed enemies. Isaacson then took the occasion to renew his demands that the US make prompt payment to his country for the damages sustained by the Israeli submarine *Meir*. The *Meir* was mildly damaged in rescuing a US foodship in the Atlantic last week.

'Here at home, the new census will indicate that the birthrate remains down by a considerable margin in our country, good news to everyone. We'll be back with the lighter side of the news and a closing word to the wise after this word from Union Carbide, makers of BreatheFree masks for your safety.'

Helen turned quickly. 'Daddy – how do you know the birthrate's down? I mean – who'd volunteer to be a census-taker?'

Ross Caudill smiled slightly. 'They do know, honey. Computers and so on. And I guess lots of people would volunteer to be census-takers. It's a way to make bread.'

She shook her head. 'Some way,' she said, and she shivered. She was staring at the TV screen, now, watching the commercial: a streetful of people in bright pastel clothing. All wore opaque dark glasses, of course, but that didn't stop them from looking glamorous and happy, walking on the street outside just as if it were the natural thing to do. Suddenly the girl in the tiger sweater sneezed, then bent coughing. No one stopped, of course, but as she sank down onto the sidewalk a Fep truck pulled in to the curb and one of them came running over.

He wrinkled his nose, then made a face and pulled down his helmet visor with its built in filtration-mask before squatting beside the girl. Suddenly another man was there too, and they looked at each other. The second man wore a small mask that covered his nose and eyes and had a mildly smiling mouth painted on it.

'Are you a doctor, sir?' the Fep asked.

The other man nodded. 'We've got to get her to a hospital fast,' he said. 'She's smothering to death.'

The Fep rose with a visible sigh. He shook his head. 'The hospitals are full, Doctor. You know how it is – that demo over on the North Side....'

The doctor gave the gasping girl a shot of something with his little excutane gun. He shook his head, then reached up to touch his mask.

'This would never have happened if she'd taken the trouble and the few dollars required to buy one of these.'

'That's one of the new improved BreatheFree masks, isn't it, with the subminiaturized air recycler and optional earguards?'

'Yes,' the doctor said. 'It filters out 87 percent of harmful pollutants in the air, and 100 percent of deadly particulates.'

'I understand they're easy to remove, too,' the Fep said. (The girl was not gasping so much, now. At least her mammoth bosom was not rising and falling with such rapidity within the tight sweater.)

'Oh yes,' the doctor said, removing the mask and replacing it quickly with obvious ease. 'Say – it *is* bad out there today.'

The Fep laughed. 'Out there?' He gestured. 'We're right here on Broadway, doctor.'

The girl was sitting up, blinking and looking around, one hand at her bosom.

'Wonder why the bastard didn't put the mask on her, temporarily,' Helen's brother Bert-Ross said.

'Sh,' Helen told him, 'because it's a commercial, dummy.'

'Oh,' the doctor said, also laughing as he glanced about. 'My new improved BreatheFree respirator is so effective, I'd forgotten. It's like being in your own home.' He turned his masked face to the girl, whose dark glasses had come off. She had very pretty blue eyes.

'Young lady, you are lucky we both happened on you. You'd better go straight to the nearest store and buy a BreatheFree mask like this one. The cost is certainly nominal – after all, your life is at stake – and they come in fourteen sizes and five delightful colors.'

'Oh thank you, Doctor – but how did you guess I was

just on my way to buy one?' she asked, and she and the doctor and the Fep laughed. They were faded out to be replaced by a very serious-looking man sitting behind a big desk. He was looking straight into Helen Caudill's eyes.

'Now you and I know that was only a demonstration with trained actors, folks, but – doesn't it make you think? Maybe you'd better call up now and have YOUR Breathe-Free delivered right to your door.'

The 'caster was back, ready to give them the Lighter Side of the News, when Mother called: Dinner was ready. Ross Caudill snicked off the TV and rose. He was always more sprightly about dinner, Helen had noticed, on grocery day than at other times.

But it was powered milk and reconstituted seawood salad and burgers, anyhow. Just last week the Seventh Day Adventists had publicly congratulated the American people for doing what they had been doing for years: eating burgers made of soybean. They had also announced that they were sending a recipe book to the White House. A day later the President had publicly thanked them, and said that both the Seventh Day Adventists and some public-minded publisher could do a great service to the American people if they would arrange to have that cookbook published in a form readily available to everyone, perhaps in paperback that could be purchased by every family in the nation for only a couple or three dollars.

And just yesterday NBC had announced its burger recipe-of-the-day program, with an Adventist as technical advisor.

'Daddy,' Helen said as they ate, loading on salt and pepper and Lea and Perrins' All-Purpose Sauce, 'I need a favor.'

He looked questioningly at her, ready to commit him self.

'The day after tomorrow I have to read my assignment aloud—'

'Honey! Wonderful! I'm proud of you!'

'Ross, you knew about it,' his wife said. 'She's known for a month, and we told you the same day she was notified.

She just didn't know until yesterday what her assignment would be.'

He gazed at her. 'Oh yeah.' He looked from Phoebe back to his daughter. 'Well, sweetheart, what's the favor? You *know* I'll get a tape so I can see my little girl lecturing a hundred million students.'

She laughed. 'Oh Daddy – it isn't for *national* college. It's just *here*.' She looked down at her plate.

'Well, that's still twenty thousand boys and girls,' her father said, and caught his wife's glance, and amended: 'young men and women.'

'Yeah,' Bert said, 'so what the hell's the favor, sister?'

Phoebe looked at him. 'Son – why don't you try to avoid using that kind of language, at least at the table?'

Bert-Ross opened his mouth, clamped it shut, and regarded his plate. Then he got up and left the table. The drama was lessened only somewhat by the fact that he'd already cleaned his plate of both first and second helpings.

After the usual silence, Ross Caudill said, 'Someday we're going to find out that damned kid's a Panther!'

'Oh Ross, don't be silly. He's just a boy, testing his wings. And cooped up like this – what do you expect?'

Ross looked seriously at his wife. 'I fully expect,' he said, 'to wake up some morning and find him gone, and to learn that he's stolen a bike or a car and become a Gyppie.'

'Ross!'

'Daddy! Honestly – he isn't anything like that!'

Ross stared at the two, his daughter and his wife. 'Yeah well, how're you going to keep 'em down in the apt after they've seen TV?'

Phoebe shook her head. 'It's a release, Ross. That's what all the psychologists are saying. As long as they're taught the dangers of going out, the TV serves to compensate for their desire to go out, or something like that. You know; if they can see it, they don't have to do it.'

'Uh-huh.'

'Oh gosh, the *clothes*,' Helen said. 'And all those people, just walking out in the air and the sun . . . but I don't believe it. Anyhow, that's the favor I need, Daddy.' She looked at him with serious brown eyes.

He looked his question at her.

'The assignment. It's to analyze a commercial as if I were on the FCC. Well, I've made up a list of all the things wrong with the one we just saw – you know, the Breathe-Free – and I wish you'd listen to it and see if I left anything out.'

He sat back smiling. 'Good grief, what's right about the damned thing? All they do is lie, lie, lie. It's like the government. Anyhow, why didn't you tell me before it came on?'

'They'll run the same one on the eleven o'clock news,' Phoebe told him.

'Which is over at eleven-thirty, and if Helen sees anything she missed she'll have to do the whole thing over – do you think she should be up that late, Phoebe?'

'Daddy, I'm SIXTEEN!'

'I know, but tomorrow you'll have to get up and go read your assignment, honey. You'll need all the rest you can get, for that. You want to be at your very best. I'd sure hate to see you lose that scholarship.'

'No danger of that,' Phoebe said, in a voice full of motherly pride. 'It's all locked up. Next year we will be receiving tapes direct from Hahvahd. Ours is the only set in the whole building that will be tuned to the finest university in the country.'

Ross said nothing. He was proud to have graduated from the University of Kentucky in the first class to attend all four years via TV. And Bert-Ross was in his second year via U of K. But after all – Harvard!

Helen was still waiting for him to OK the favor when they heard the crash. Ross jumped; Helen bit her lip; Phoebe sighed.

'It's Bert-Ross,' she said. 'Practicing his karate again.'

Her husband sighed. 'Damned kid,' he muttered, 'he could try to be more careful.' But he said nothing more; after all, anyone who couldn't defend himself would probably be dead the first time he stepped out the door. It hadn't been three days since Ross had had to ballkick that punk with the knife and the hungry eyes who'd somehow got into the basement garage to wait for someone to come home from work.

Chapter Ten

'To begin with,' Helen Caudill said, or rather read from the piece of paper notably quivering in her hand, 'I cannot comment on the totally ridiculous dialog in the commercial presentation under study. That of course was designed to sell the product, and we were witnessing a clearly defined commercial. The rule is that ancient one applied to fantasy: one must first accept the premise, which is that people on the street attempt to persuade one another to use this or that product. In so doing, they employ the language of Madison Avenue.

'The dialog was clearly in full accord with the Dramatic License in Advertisements and Commercial Presentations Act.'

She looked up, wetting her lips in a clever attempt to call attention away from her hands, slipping the first sheet of paper under the others. She'd picked that up from her Tellyschool teachers.

'We were shown a large and heterogeneous group of people, all walking along the street of an obviously large city. I submit, to begin with, that they would not all have looked so glamorous, nor would they have appeared so happy. It just . . . it just isn't that way. Next we focused on a young woman. Her attire was totally unbelievable. She was wearing a very tight sweater. No one would go out that way. No one would dare, not even right in the middle of the downtown island, in the business district. She was attracting too much attention to herself, and that is dangerous. As Desmond Morris once wrote, "Why refrigerate a room and then light a fire in it?" '

'Honey – does that really fit, right there?' Phoebe Caudill was frowning.

Helen put her head on one side with a little smile. 'Well . . . it's a good place for a quotation, and it almost fits. Morris was talking about his, in his time, women covered the bosom for reasons they thought of as "moral" or "religious," but then called attention to the concealed bosom by wearing – under the concealing clothing – a brassiere that exaggerated their shape.'

'Wellll . . . if you think you need a quotation in there . . . I think you're doing fine, baby.'

Ross Caudill nodded, indulging in that sublimely ridiculous paternal affliction known as beaming.

Helen smiled, looked a bit shy, just a bit, and then started to resume her reading.

There was a thunderous explosion and both Helen and her mother clutched their breasts; Helen squeaked. Ross cursed. 'Bastards. Busting the damned sound barrier, that's all they think about. The screens blot out the jets . . . but DAMN those supersonic planes!'

After a moment, Helen, her heart still pounding, coninued. 'The Feps arrived—'

'Shouldn't you be more formal, sweetheart?'

Helen considered, then nodded. 'The Federal Policemen arrived awfully fast, but I guess that could happen. Hm. The Federal Policemen reached the scene with incredible rapidity, but that is probably possible in some circumstances.' She looked up questioningly.

'Oh, beautiful,' her mother said.

'But – then came the physician, bending at once over the young woman. A doctor, a physician, stopping unbidden to help someone? Now I must admit that that is merely silly. Not since the middle of the century have medical men dared do so. A physician, just stopping to help someone that way, taking the risk of being mugged, and undergoing the old risk, the bane of his profession, of a malpractice suit should the young woman not regain perfect health?' She shook her head. 'No. This one incident throws the whole commercial into the area of the ridiculous, and I submit that viewers all over the country laughed at that point and missed a great deal of the subsequent development of the manufacturer's message.'

She glanced up; both her parents were nodding.

'Finally, I believe this, *if* we accept the foregoing unacceptable premise. The physician certainly should have and would have placed his own mask on the girl, even if for just a minute. Long enough for it to help the shot he gave her to take effect.'

After a moment, Helen said, 'That's all.'

Her father applauded. Her mother smiled, nodding.

'I think it's really good, honey, and I'm sure it's all there,' Phoebe said.

'Some of the language was a little flowery—' Ross began.

'Strange,' Phoebe said, 'I was just going to suggest that she tone it up a little.'

They all laughed: 'Well,' Ross Caudill said, spreading his hands, 'That's the whole point, isn't it? Ya can't please 'em all!'

While Helen sat working over perfecting the prose of her presentation to her classmates, her father went in to talk with his son. There was an argument, of course. Helen heard Bert-Ross quote Sartre's line about his father's having had the decency and good judgment to die when Sartre was young and take his long shadow off his son's life. Phoebe gasped. Then there were definite sounds of a scuffle from the next room, and Phoebe rushed from the little living room.

Helen sat listening, her head up, frowning. What was that Jefferson Andrews had said in his last book? He'd been quoting or paraphrasing the old pioneer-writer, the instinctivist Robert Ardrey. He'd said the age of anxiety was an uncertain period of transition in the adolescence of man, when old superstitions and incorrect 'knowledge' had ceased being enough but when the full comprehension of maturity hadn't yet come. Helen's lips moved. She was a very good student, and had made notes and a report, and had committed some of the words to memory without even realizing it.

'"In such an awkward emotional age we lose faith in fathers, divine or domestic, and yearn for more suitable stars to steer by."'

Helen nodded, she wasn't sure whether that was Andrews or Ardrey speaking; she'd have to look it up. But she remembered the last line:

'Maturity must come.'

I wonder if I'll go through the same thing, she wondered, and then jerked up and around as angry footsteps came into the room.

It was not her father. It was Bert-Ross, his eyes angry and his face set tightly, teeth clenched. He went straight to the door and fumbled, then cursed as its complicated locking system resisted angry hands.

'Bert-Ross! Bert! No – where are you going?'

'Out.' And he got the door open, and banged it after him.

Helen ran after him. She felt a moment of fear in the hallway outside, but after all it was her own apartment building, and the people of one's own building came first after one's family. Trust must begin somewhere, someone had said recently; let it begin within the building in which we live as strangers to our neighbors. She ran after her brother. Down the narrow hall with its bright lights and rows of locked doors; a tunnel through locked, sealed, soundproof humanity.

When she rounded the corridor corner he was already entering the elevator.

'Bert-Ross!'

'Go back, you damned silly girl!'

She slapped the button; the doors ceased closing, jerked, quivered, rolled back. She faced her brother's bright and angry eyes at a distance of three feet.

'Bert . . . come back. You can't—'

'I am damned tired of being told what I can't. Now even you've started. Well, you stay here and suck up to those damned dinosaurs, and eat the lousy soybean guck that's all *he* can afford. He hates me, he doesn't hear a damned thing I say, and he doesn't give a damn what I do. Well, I don't either. He's stupid, stupid, stupid, Helen. He and his kind made this godawful world, and I'm getting the hell OUT!'

'Bert! They'll KILL YOU OUT THERE!'

But the doors were already closing. He'd hit the inner Override switch, provided for the safety of the apt-dwellers, and probably didn't even hear her last words.

She was sobbing hysterically when her mother and father came to draw her back into their own apt. None of the other doors opened.

MEANWHILE: VI

A City Is Bad Enough in the Daytime, But at Night It's a Cave Full of Snakes

Rather than raise the big vehicle door on the basement garage, Bert-Ross Caudill peered out through the one-way glass of the little pedestrian door. Then he opened it and stepped out; Out. It was very brightly lit outside, now the lights were encaged in a steel grill with one-by-one centimeter interstices. The light had been replaced forty-one times before someone in the apt, on the third floor, Bert-Ross remembered, had gone around taking up a collection to have the rip-proof shields installed.

Bert-Ross took exactly four steps before the dark shape rose up from behind the base of the light pole. Bert-Ross' heart seemed to jump violently. His lip and hands shuddered. His throat was suddenly intensely dry, tight, feeling as if he'd swallowed a handful of lint. He stared at the dark-clothed, man-shape. It held something that glittered in the light.

'Hey big boy. Whatcha doing out here all by yourself?'

'Getting the hell out,' Bert-Ross said. And then he realized, and he added, 'joining you.' He tried very hard to make his voice sound firm and fearless, cocky, as if he belonged outside. He didn't glance up as the big jet shrieked over.

'Yeah? Where's your weapon, stupid? Joining me, huh?'

'I mean everybody outside.'

The other boy chuckled his sneer. (He was a boy, less than twenty, as Bert-Ross was, although his face was invisible because the light was directly above him.)

'So he had a row with his daddy, did he, and left the nice cool comfy cozy apt for the big wide world, huh? Well, there's enough people out here, kiddyboy, and we don't need no more company. Now you just gonna have to give me whatever you got in your pockets, and then either get back inside or run like hell, kiddyboy.'

Bert-Ross stared. His eyes flicked down to the knife, back up to the invisible face, a blackness with a small white patch: the jut of the other boy's nose. He was scared. He was unarmed, an apt-dweller all his life, and this other had spent god knows how many years running the streets, sleeping in alleys and behind apts, waiting for someone to be stupid enough to come out alone and unarmed.

But Bert-Ross had been full of anger and adrenalin when he left his "comfy cozy" apt, and he was still adrenalized, both with anger and fear. His eyes narrowed. He edged away from the building; he didn't want his back against it.

The other youth came quickly forward, legs bent easily in a practiced crouch. Bert-Ross had to back – toward the building.

'Easy, kiddyboy. Don't do anything nutty, like tryina run. You got no idea how fast I am – I haven't had enough food to put any fat on, like you. Listen, I tell you what – maybe we can make a team. You just take me back inside, that's all. You can get in, I can't. I don't know the numbers and the door doesn't know my voice. OK?'

Bert-Ross considered, but shook his head. He didn't give a damn; he almost wished he could get this baboon together with the old man. But – not with his mother, or Helen. God, no.

An incoming jet roared over so low his ears rang and he felt his heart leap.

The other youth advanced.

Speed, simultaneous actions, all occurring faster than words can be slapped onto paper, one letter at a time. Bert-Ross reached into his pocket to see if there was anything there he might use for defense. This was immediately interpreted a little more strongly: that he was grasping a weapon. The baboon charged, swinging the knife up and out. Bert-Ross dodged instinctively, and he was far from fat, and because of his dreams he had practiced daily for years, especially the last two. The knife flashed past and Bert-Ross heard it grate against the cement wall behind him and the boy's curse as he missed and maybe injured his knife and his knuckles to boot, and Bert-Ross turned, swinging, beside him now and facing the opposite way, and his flat-held hand came around in a rushing arc that terminated in the back of the other's neck.

The baboon grunted and made an uglier sound as his face snapped forward into the wall. The knife clattered. He sagged against the building, hands swinging down, and started folding.

His face left a dark smear as it slid down the cement wall.

Bert-Ross stared panting down at him. God, could he have – had he – was the night-creature – dead? Was it possible? Could he have had an encounter so suddenly, so soon (of course; there was always somebody waiting outside apts, all day and all night. They merely faded when a patrol came by and resumed their positions seconds later). And – could he have *won?*

He raised his hand, looked at it. Thought about Bob Strong on TV, and the endless karate lessons and demonstrations, his own endless watching and listening and practicing and thinking.

Yes. He had, and he stood taller. He had won. The attacker still lay in a rumpled, wrinkled little heap. A foot away from him was his knife. It appeared to have an intact point; it must not have been broken against the wall. Bert-Ross looked at it, licking his lips. Then he looked swiftly around. Again. Went to one knee. Looked around again.

He picked up the knife.

He tested point and blade, and jerked back his hand – sharp! Deadly sharp. He shuddered. This nasty little six-inch blade had come straight at him, very nearly sunk right into him. And he had – he had....

Bert-Ross Caudill clutched the naked knife tightly in his hand. Then he turned and walked away from the body; dead or unconscious, it was neither his business nor of concern to him. He walked down the driveway and out onto the sidewalk, looked both ways, chose one and started walking. There was a new spring in his step, a step of confidence, of pride.

It was a swagger.

Chapter Eleven

Ross Caudill didn't call the police; his wife did. She was weeping when she made the call, waiting and waiting for the crisp answer because they were so busy, and she managed to get herself stopped during the conversation with the quiet-voiced, matter-of-fact man on the other end. But she was weeping again when she switched off the phone.

He hadn't seemed *interested*. (There were three hundred thousand people in the city. It was a small town. It was not a complete jungle, such as New York, but it was working on it.)

He had been so matter-of-fact. (He had told her that hers was the hundred and third such call from a parent that week, and it was only Friday. At least her missing offspring was a boy.)

He had said he would report the information to Fep. (FPF hadn't the time to cruise about examining faces and attempting to match them against many weeks of a hundred and three missing persons by Friday evening. FPF had more important things to do. They did always contact the parents or wives or husbands or whatever when they found the bodies, assuming they were identifiable and had been reported. On the other hand they didn't bother to try identifying or calling anyone about the bodies of molesters; Gyppies or rippers or muggers or baboons.)

He had not said so in so many words, but he had indicated to her, quietly, that her son would in all probability not survive the night. (A Presidential Task Force had recently come up with a percentage on that, in the course of its study into related Urban Problems. There were many Bert-Ross Caudills, male and female, who could not seem to resist the call of Outside. Perhaps they found it glamorous, for some unknown reason, and the Task Force asked for more money to look into that. Perhaps they just needed to get out from between the walls within the shelter of which their parents had raised them, protected them, taught them, loved them. And they seemed to go Out at the slightest excuse; reasons seldom seemed rational. But at any rate, the chances for surviving the first night, for a young apt-raised male – as opposed to a slum-dweller or the son of a garink – were precisely one in four point two. Apparently that was halved within twenty-four hours; some coped. They stayed out there until they ran afoul of Feps or others like them, existing on the streets.)

He had asked if Bert-Ross had had weapons, and when she had said no, terrified, he had made a small sad sound. Discussion unnecessary.

She turned from the phone to gaze with helpless, tear-glittering eyes at her husband. He was staring at the TV. Helen was in the other room, sobbing.

'Ross. . . .'

He looked angrily up at her. 'Phoebe, dammit, there's nothing we can DO! We CAN'T go out there looking for him! It's his bed, let him lie in it!'

'Ross—' She stood helplessly, looking as she felt, grievously small and female and helpless and solace-seeking. And her husband stared at the TV, and she knew he wasn't looking at it, knew he didn't mean what he said, knew he wished it hadn't happened, that his son were here watching the screen too, that things were different . . . but he couldn't say so. He was a man, and his territorial limits had shrunk to next to nothing, this tiny apt and the tiny minik in which he drove to the tiny desk in the tiny cubicle in which he worked.

He and she had had only two children, merely replacing themselves. They did not overeat or overproduce, and she didn't even own an electric can-opener. Their bottles went down the chute to melt and recycle and be carted off and returned to the soil or factory. They had raised their two children, and taught them, done their best. This world wasn't of their making. They had tried. They didn't waste.

They didn't pollute. They minded their own business. They didn't bother with status symbols, which everyone said were wrong. They just . . . lived. And her son Ross was a *good* boy.

Then why him?

MEANWHILE: VII

A City Is Like A Forest. Who Can See Each Tree In It, and Furthermore Who Gives A Damn?

Helen Caudill's notes toward an essay, *Seeking a Better World.*

Ardrey, Robert, *The Territorial Imperative*:

'As important as territory to social animals – and we may someday find that it is more important – is the compulsion to achieve status within one's society, Territory is essentially defensive, an inward mechanism aiding us to defend what we have; status is essentially aggressive, an inward pressure. . . .'

Hardin, Garrett, *The Tragedy of the Commons* (article: *Science*):

'The only way we can preserve and nurture other and more precious freedoms is by relinquishing the freedom to breed, and that very soon.'

Fannin, Clarke, *Why does the Underground Press Carry So Many* DARLING PLEASE COME HOME *Ads?* (article: *Ramparts*, 1976):

'Take away a man's territory, baby, and you got an unhappy man. But lift his *status*, and then what have you got? You've got an *impotent* man, jim, and Junior just can't respect or hang onto no impotent daddy. Now you keep on cramming daddy into jobs the size of a chimp's brain and dad himself into an "apartment" the size of a jail cell, and the kids'll just keep on leaving, and the LA *Freep* will keep on running all those COME HOME JUNIOR ads and the LA pigs will just keep on cramming junior into apartment-sized jail cells. And you can BELIEVE that, Amerikkka!'

Andrews, Jefferson, *Quo in Arco Vadimus*?, '96.

'The distinguished secretary for Health, Education and mostly Welfare says that crime is a result of poverty and environment and upbringing. And I say, with a few reservations, male bovine defecation, which the dist. sec. can look up and improve his mind. The d.s. is a behaviorist, and the problem with behaviorists is the same as that which resulted in the errors in Desmond Morris' otherwise excellent book, *The Naked Ape*.

'Morris couldn't explain everything by zoology, ignoring psychology and (learned) behaviorism, no matter how hard he tried. Now the distinguished secretary of H.E. (m) W. has a job to do and he has to get down on his knees and bare his genitals and beg Congress for more money every year because that is where it is At, statusly speaking, up on the Potomac. He *has* to explain everything according to modern psychological knowledge and the behavioral school. And the poor devil is utterly ignoring biology.

'Some say that the demos (they were called "riots" and "demonstrations," then, apparently interchangeable) that forced us to close our colleges and outlaw public gatherings so that baseball games are played to empty stands – and that forced, eventually, the creation of FPF – were a result of a man named Spock, a physician. He was the Bible for a generation of American parents. He taught permissiveness: just let Junior do whatever he wants, folks, and used applied psychology. (My grandfather was at the same time applying a large psychology book, by a fellow named Havelock Ellis, to the seat of my father's pants.) Well, that may well be *part* of the answer. The psychological and learned-behavior answer, the answer for those who look at man with a Pavlovian eye.

'We had a thing in this country once called the Great Depression, and I am not referring to the little setback in the early seventies. The Great Depression has *never* been described or characterized as a period of great crime. (Do not remind me of the current revival of *The Untouchables*. That is *organized* crime, which is like war, and we are discussing disorganized crime, which is like the kid down the block and the man next door.) The crime rate during the Great Depression couldn't hold a candle to that of the war-prosperity decade of the sixties, which can't hold an M-20 to the crime rate of our present era.

'Where does that put poverty as a root-cause for crime?

'Now Mr. Morris did say some highly intelligent things in his best-known book. Among them was that "the best solution for ensuring world peace is the widespread promotion of contraception or abortion. . . . Contraception is obviously preferable, and any religious or other "moralizing" factions that oppose it must face the fact that they are engaged in dangerous war-mongering.' (British spellings courtesy Imperative, territorial, and Phobia, xeno.)

'Mr. Morris *said* that sardine-tin overpopulation would create tensions and stresses that would rip apart our societies long before it succeeded in starving us to death. Sure enough, here we are. I recommend Mr. Morris to the distinguished secretary's attention. I urge him to attempt to understand the link between what he calls "Urban problems" and the current and apparently permanent lack of such niceties as clams and oysters from down Florida way. Our lack of those fine "luxury foodstuffs" derives from the presence of a nasty little invader down there called the Red Tide (no kin to McCarthy or the popular pollutant): *G.breve*, and ciguatera poison.

'It would seem that I am arguing behaviorism; that is, learned behaviorism. We overbreed, therefore we overeat, overspread, and grow lovely little red tides to decorate the Gulf Coast. It is true. I am saying just that, and it is nothing new. But even overbreeding, you see, is an *effect*, not a cause. As to the present crime rate – what a ridiculous term! We should begin to refer to the "uncriminal elements" among us, since they appear to form a deathly-silent minority.

'Readers should witness the animal and utterly barbaric assiduousness with which this writer defends his land. His . . . territory. *His* land. His. His territory, and he has an ancient instinctual imperative to defend it, to increase and multiply that it might be defended after his death, to think first of his territory and then of his wife and then of his family and *then,* perhaps, of defending the distinguished secretary of HEW. What we are dealing with is *biology.* Zoology. Instinct, if you will, or "drives" if you prefer euphemisms. We are dealing with the territorial imperative, and with the great human desire to sink, which is a euphemism for fuck. That is something the distinguished secretary should understand; he and his ilk have been doing it to the country for years.

'Who possesses territory in our cities? And should we count a cubicle called an apartment, a cave in the midst of a great complex of identical caves soaring into the sky, protected with unopenable outer doors and locked inner doors and iron screens over the windows – when there are windows?' Animals live in those caves, naked apes, if you will. But they don't have any territory, and thus they don't have any respect for themselves, and they certainly don't get it from their offspring.

'In many societies of the lower animals – you remember the lower animals – copulation is engaged in in so-called "arenas." That is, the males fight to stake out a piece of real estate, and the females come to them. (Seriously. Look it up.) *Only those males reproduce.* And the ones with the best territories, the harder-to-defend ones, enjoy the most copulation. The others simply don't reproduce.

'As we see it, our society is set up on precisely opposite lines. The further in the sites, the more deeply buried within cities and apts, the more easily defended they are and the less choice territories they constitute. They survive. And they breed.

'What do they breed?

'Crime, that's what.'

Chapter Twelve

On the fourth day after his son's disappearance Ross Caudill had the locks and codes of his apt changed. He also advised the manager, and that evening there was a special apartment meeting – channel one, reserved for closed-circuit communications. Bert-Ross Caudill was not mentioned, but the manager announced the new codes for the outside doors, effective immediately. Every effort was made to contact Mr. and Mrs. Emery Brower, who were out that evening. They were never seen again. Presumably they had returned home, been unable to get the doors to open for them, and had been ripped off right there in their minik.

After waiting five days in accord with the law, the manager leased their apt to the first name on his waiting list.

That was on the ninth day after Ross Caudill's disappearance.

The Caudills watched television practically all the time now, and while none of them said anything overt, they all three bent forward and strained their eyes as they searched among mob-scene faces for Bert-Ross.

He was (apparently) not involved in the demo at the East Gate, when a huge gang of homeless baboons tried to rip off a convoy of five big trucks. The trucks seemed well armed, and the announcer commented on the (unidentified) young sharpshooter in the first truck, which passed into the city intact and escaped the ensuing demo. The baboons were of course attacked by others, called 'outraged citizens.'

The result was a melee involving first hundreds, then thousands.

One of the trucks was overturned to spew its precious cargo all over the street. Local police and Feps arrived within ten minutes after the firing of the first shot, but by that time hundreds were dead or wounded and a small war was in progress, involving an "estimated" thirteen or fourteen thousand persons of "all walks of life".

Via their loudspeakers, the armored Fep vehicles gave their required warning. Perhaps it was heard by a thousand or so of the combatants, perhaps more or less. A Fepcopter puttered overhead, repeating the warning. A volley was fired into the air. The demo continued, its noise nearly as loud as that of the jet the TV sound-recorder picked up and passed on.

The Feps then of course lowered their guns and fired, from three directions simultaneously, into the crowd for a period of one minute.

After that the remainder of the crowd dispersed, raggedly. Official estimates placed the dead at just under two thousand, the badly wounded at thirteen or fourteen hundred, and the otherwise injured at between two and three thousand. Approximately 10 percent of the food from the overturned truck was salvaged, although no one could be sure how much had been eaten on the spot or carried off by fleeing rioters. Over half of it was merely trampled down in the street.

Ross Caudill's stomach rumbled. 'Bastards! If I'd been there—' He broke off. Yes. If I'd been there.

If he'd been there he'd have joined thousands of others in righteously indignant attack on the attackers. But Fep bullets were not equipped with discriminatory homing device that guided them only into bonafide card-carrying baboons.

'Why are they called baboons?' Phoebe wondered aloud, blinking and squeezing her eyes tight shut. She had been staring, straining to see if her son was in the demo.

'Because that's what they are,' her husband growled. 'Filthy dirty baboons.'

'It came from the chacma baboons,' Helen said, as if she were in an old rote-school. Her eyes were often faraway these days, her voice often wistful, singsong. 'Vice president whatsisname came up with the phrase, back in the seventies. He was speaking about the population problem and all the student demos then, and he said that aggressive baboons who kept picking fights usually got hurt. They'd be left behind, because baboons are like Gyppies, always moving. And then the bad one would get himself eaten, which was a good thing, because that way society maintained order and discipline and only the orderly, disciplined members reproduced.'

Her mother looked at her. 'Really? Is that where it came from?'

Helen nodded. Ross patted her head. 'That's my brilliant TV-star daughter,' he said. He had played the tape of her televised assignment over and over.

Helen sighed. 'Oh *look*.'

They looked. Another special report; this time on the non-city dwellers. They were in the helicopter, swinging well above trees and fields, and Helen gasped as she saw a herd of twenty or so black and white animals. She was told they were Holstein cattle, big milk producers. And those brown ones were Jerseys, who gave rather less milk but whose milk was richer in butterfat.

'Polysaturated,' Phoebe commented. She had developed quite a belly, even on burgers.

They saw children in the fields, and men and women, dressed *differently*. It was often hard to be certain if they were looking at women and girls or not, so many of them wore long pants and broad-brimmed hats. Now and then, though, Helen saw bare brown legs and unconsciously hugged herself, identifying with girls her age out there among all those trees and amid all that grass, growing their own food and often having their own bedrooms.

'These are small farmers,' the announcer told them. 'Some of them sell a little food or milk, others merely grow enough to provide for themselves and to trade with their neighbors. One man, for instance, might raise milk-cows and graincrops exclusively, while a neighbor has chickens. These people thus trade both foodstuffs and labor.'

'Bastards,' Ross muttered. 'Living out there on all that land, with all that space – and all that *food*! It's obscene, and here we are crammed together, half-starving!'

'Oh Ross, we aren't *starving*.'

'Cows,' he said, 'are where beef comes from. How long since you've tasted beef?'

'Only three weeks ago, Ross Caudill!'

'Well . . . in New York City some of them go forever, all their lives, without even seeing a piece of beef.'

Phoebe sighed, gazing at the screen. 'Then we're not so

bad off, at that. But it does look wonderful, doesn't it?'

He didn't answer.

'Daddy? Why couldn't we – have you ever thought of – of moving? Of going out somewhere, you know, way Out, and getting a job, or trying to buy some land? I'd be glad to raise corn and things, chickens even, and I'll bet Mother would too. Think of all the *space*.'

'Look!' Phoebe's arm snapped up. 'A bird. What's that blue bird – how *beautiful*! Is that a bluebird?'

'I think that's a jay,' Helen said wistfully. 'I've seen pictures, and it looked like he had a crest.'

'Awful, raucous-voiced things,' her father said in the reclining chair behind her, and she sighed. 'Lord no, I haven't ever thought of moving out of the city! I wouldn't know the first thing about farmwork – and it's *hard* work, believe you me! No, I guess your mother's right, sweetheart. We're not so bad off after all.'

'These people,' the announcer told them, 'are envied their idyllic pastoral existence, living out their lives in very much the same manner as their grandfathers did, a hundred years ago. All is not peace and birdsong tranquility, though. . . .' And he went on to tell them about the vicissitudes of non-city life, of the tremendous dependency on weather, the dangers of insects and reptiles and so on.

And then the voice changed, and they were advised that they were about to see something totally extraordinary, a television first.

'The life of the non-city dweller is fraught with another peril, too,' the announcer's voice said, and they were shown a sprawling city from an increasingly greater height. Then they swept down to see the lines of vehicles leaving it – with nearly as many coming in. The helicopter they seemed to be in passed over a massed group of some thirty motorbikes, and Helen realized she was seeing Gyppies, the scourge of the country. Several of them looked up, shaking their fists and shouting. The camera swiftly left them and her father chuckled.

'I'll bet they had to cut out that cameraman's getting a finger,' he said, and Phoebe tried to wither him with a reproachful look and a glance at Helen. Ross sighed and replied with a she's-got-to-learn-someday shrug.

Besides, Helen had giggled. She knew what a finger was. Kids knew everything, these days. That's what TV was for. You can't keep much back from kids or kid them along much about things, when the TV's always there to cram their minds with knowledge, both positive and negative.

The next scene they saw made them all gasp. The copter swung down over another lovely area of fields and trees, then in toward a large farmhouse that looked as though it could use a coat of paint and some repairs to the porch. There were three cars in front of the place.

Sprawling out of the open door of one of the cars was a body, a youngish-looking man or boy with a dropped rifle at his fingertips. There were dark spots – holes – in the door, and the car window was shattered. Beside the porch lay another body, and Helen made a throaty little moaning noise as she saw that it was a boy of ten or twelve, wearing a long-sleeved shirt and jeans and longish hair. There was a big red flower on the front of his shirt; blood. The copter swung around the house, passing over another body: city this time, with a red puddle growing out beneath and around him.

Suddenly a girl came running out of the house. Long hair flew out behind her; Helen had noticed that these non-city people often had longer hair and didn't seem concerned with unattractivizing themselves. Her clothing was torn. There was a red streak on her cheek. Her mouth was wide open and her eyes looked like marbles, big and round and glassy.

Across the porch and the yard raced a boy, shirt-tail flapping. A gun flapped, too, at his hip. They saw him tackle her.

The screen went black; they were advised that the ensuing scene had been of such a nature as to be non-broadcastable.

When the picture returned, immediately after the announcement, Helen knew that some time had passed. The girl was all alone in the yard, now, lying very still, in an insane abandoned-doll position. She wasn't quite naked; she was covered just enough (and one knee was upbent) so that she could be shown on TV. She was smeared with blood; there was no FCC ruling about that, of course.

Helen's hands clutched each other, the palms sliding about in their own sweat, the fingers twisting and wriggling, tangling and untangling to link again. Her teeth were sunk into her lower lip.

'Oooh, *god*,' she said. The words emerged as little more than a gasp.

'Ross – Helen shouldn't—'

But Phoebe broke off as another scene-shift showed them the same house, in flames. Loaded with booty, the rippers were pulling away in their three cars.

'Wanton destruction,' the announcer said in his quiet baritone. 'Five people slain, both the mother and daughter assaulted and molested, and now the rippers leave. The house burns to the ground; the garden is trampled into waste. The rippers were not even homesteaders, as is sometimes the case. Occasionally a farm will be ripped off by people who then settle there and claim it as their own.'

'Oh *god*,' Phoebe muttered.

The cars, seen from the rear, were growing on the screen.

'Because of the immensity of this crime, slaying honest people who take little but work the land, producing food and requiring nothing in the way of food or aid, our heli-cameraman directed his pilot to drop down close behind the rippers, to note carefully the numbers on their tags and, if possible, their faces.'

The second car in the little caravan had no back window. Suddenly a black gunbarrel was thrust through the aperture, leveled directly at Helen's face. She winced and squeaked as it flashed fire at her. Then she was seeing trees – from the side, then the sky – from below, then a swift fleeting vision of the three cars again, then trees-sky-ground and there was the beginning of a crack across the screen and then nothing.

The screen was black for a moment, uncracked. She had seen the camera smash.

'The farm you saw was that of Ivan Patton and his wife and three children,' the announcer's quiet voice said. The screen showed a sky whose blueness was broken here and there by fluffy white clouds like medicine-bottle cotton. 'Ivan Patton and his wife and three children are dead. The films, everything you've seen in this special report, were taken by WSEZ-TV cameraman Bert Gardiner. His telecopter was piloted by James Rose Yancey. Bert Gardiner and James Rose Yancey are dead in the wreckage of the copter, shot down by the rippers.

'Ladies and gentlemen of the television audience, those rippers are still at large.'

Silence. White clouds on a blue sky. Fadeout.

Helen sat on the floor by her father's chair with her arms wrapped arouid her upraised knees. Her head was on her forearms; she wept softly.

'Dammit, they shouldn't show stuff like that on TV,' Ross Caudill said as he bent forward to stroke his daughter's shoulder.

And the next day he said, 'A farm is a great place to see on TV, but I'd sure hate to have to live out there like that!'

Chapter Thirteen

'So you're the young man who shoots so well, are you?'

'Yes sir.'

The man's brows rose. Slowly, he smiled. 'God! And you say *sir*? I can't imagine how long it's been since I've heard a fellow your age use that – how old are you?'

'If I'm eighteen I can be hired and paid man's wages, is that right?'

George Taylor grinned. He leaned back, reaching up to slip an index finger inside his old-fashioned clear glasses to scratch the corner of his eyebrow. 'That's right.'

'I'm eighteen.'

'More like sixteen. . . . You have a card?'

'Yes sir.' The youth didn't move to display his ID.

'Umm . . . well. You'll get a man's wage for that escort job, whether you're twelve or thirty. It was strictly your shooting that got that truck through the gates and here so that it completely missed the whole damned demo. Apparently you scared hell out of those filthy rippers. We owe you plenty – the *city* owes you a debt, for that undamaged truckload of food. Where are you from?'

'Away.' The boy waved his hand.

Taylor shook his head. 'What happens if I ask you your name? More evasions?'

The boy shrugged. 'With four hundred million people in the country? I'm Scott Andrews.'

'Scotty?'

The boy shrugged.

'Scotty, thanks. And I want to sign you on, Scotty. You must be looking for work, to've signed on as a guard on a food truck.' Taylor sighed and waved a hand flecked with brownish spots amid the hair. He seemed to have more of it on his hand than on his head, Scott thought. But then so many people were bald or fast getting that way, these days. And so many started even before they were twenty. Pollution? Evolution? No one seemed sure. It was being studied of course. Government grants were always available.

A jet went over noisily and Taylor went over to drop the soundproof, pollution-proof screen over the window. He forefingered the background noiser.

'I just wanted . . . to see a city,' Scott Andrews said.

Taylor turned to stare at him. 'Farmboy, huh? Well, I guess I can understand. Farmers have it pretty rough, pretty rough. And thank god for 'em. About seven percent of the population's feeding the rest of us, now. That means one man feeds fourteen and a half others, who keep the industry going and the cities from falling apart. I understand they're up to a one for six ratio in Russia, they've raised the personal-acerage allotment over there. Nothing like a man and his land . . . but a boy just naturally gets itchy for the bright lights and tall buildings, doesn't he?'

'Yes sir.'

'Sir.' Taylor shook his head again. 'Well, Scott Andrews. You're in the city, and your baptism was with fire. We lost one whole truck out of that convoy of food. That's a lot of empty bellies, or a lot of not-as-well-filled ones, anyhow. But you saved the first truck, and from what Paul says your shooting demoralized the rippers so bad, that probably saved us having a lot more food dumped or stolen and eaten, or black-marketed by thieves. I've got a convoy of three trucks leaving for Cincinnati in the morning. Five a.m. You want to be in the lead truck?'

'No sir, I don't think I do.' At Taylor's look of shocked surprise at having a flat job offered turned down, Scott bit his lip. 'I took that job to get myself here. It was transportation.' He smiled. He had pale eyes, pale eyebrows, pale hair, like evening sunlight on old straw. 'And it's sure nice to get paid for the ride, instead of payin' for it.'

'But – what ARE you going to do? Where're you going to STAY?'

'I don't know. I'll find a place.' The boy's eyes were steady.

Taylor stared at him a moment before rising – his chair squeaked – and walking over to the barred window. He squinted through the grimy safety glass. It was clean on the inside, but glass got grimy fast, outside. Taylor Hauling wasn't exactly in a residential district.

He turned back to the youngster with the broad old belt slung from his left hip to his right thigh, where the holster seemed to cling to his leg. From the holster protruded the dark butt of a revolver. In guiding Taylor's lead truck through the East Gate, past the crowd of rippers that had somehow been ready, had somehow known the convoy was coming, Scott Andrews had proven he was emphatically, frighteningly capable of using that revolver.

'Son . . . you've gotta have a place to stay, and you've got to have a job.' Taylor raised his arms, spreading his hands. 'Hell, I can find you an apt or a room somewhere, no sweat. And the job's here. Three-fifty a week, plus meals when you're out of town.'

'Which would be most of the time.'

'Well . . . about half and half.'

Scott shook his head. 'Can you use me here in town?'

Taylor squeezed his jaw with his hand, looking pained. 'Sure. But not at that kind of money. Look, Scotty, you're a Shotgun! You proved it on that truck at the East Gate. You—'

Scott leaned forward across Taylor's desk as the trucker settled back into his chair. It protested shrilly.

'Mr Taylor – the point is I'm just not interested in making killing my life's work. My dad has killed, and my brother and mother too. They have to, sometimes. Everybody has to, that's the way the world is. I understand about population pressure, and territory too. But I don't want killing to be my *business*.'

'Scotty,' Taylor said, shaking his head, 'You've just made it clear you're a bright kid. Educated. Now I don't know what the hell you're doing here, what you're running away from. I don't much care. You're a hero in Lexington, and a hero to *me*. Now listen, because you're bright, and consider money and odds and your future.' George Taylor leaned toward the youth, who straightened to regard him with those ingenuous blue-gray eyes. They were a little like ice on a bright-skied day in winter; a little hard and cold, and perfectly steady. Taylor looked away from him; a man just didn't look straight into another's eyes when he spoke. Men never had. Those few who had done so had made others uncomfortable – while judging others by themselves: *if he can't look me square in the eye I can't trust him.* The one-way dark glasses had solved that, as well as giving a man a feeling of privacy. No one could look into his eyes. Nor could he look into theirs. Taylor wished to hell he'd had his glasses on when Paul brought this kid in. Those eyes were disconcerting, a little shuddery and scary. Taylor didn't like the feeling that they were staring right into him, examining his very private innards.

'Scotty, this's the first trouble – the first *real* trouble, I mean, on any of my trucks in six weeks. I have eight trucks, and they move all over the country. Now you figure the odds of being Shotgun on one of my trucks; does that sound like making a career of killing?'

Scotty shook his head. 'No sir, it doesn't,' he said, running his left hand down the thigh of his jeans. 'But would you tell me what you start a driver off at? Money, I mean? Startin' wage?'

'Can you drive, too?'

'No sir. Not like Paul, anyhow. He came through town the same way he handled that rig on the highway. Well, almost,' he said, remembering how Paul had switched to the electric engine as they approached the city gates. When the rippers had appeared and the boy beside him had – with seeming calm – dropped his window and started firing, Paul had put the truck back on the highway engine, the death-breathing gasoline motor, and jammed his foot down. He hadn't switched back to electric until they were well within the city and his radio had crackled and a Fep voice had warned him. He'd forgotten, in the excitement. He had probably run down five or six of the rippers. Scott didn't care to remember how many he had shot down, easily, sitting in the seat beside Paul with the window open and inviting death. But Paul had told him, a little awed, as they tooled through town and pulled in to Taylor's docks: Rippers just weren't accustomed to being opened up on by someone with a gun – who could use it.

There'd been a trial just last year, in which two rippers had sued a man who had shot the third member of their trio, and killed him. He had been their brother.

'We were just *throwing* bricks,' one of the baboons had said, and people had looked at each other, and then the defense attorney had set up a sheet of safety glass and cracked it with the first brick and shattered it with the second, all before the judge could stop him. The judge had been angry, but the point had been made. The trial was over. Bricks could be met with guns, although the law was still a little nebulous as to the distance involved. A bullet was far more effective at longer ranges, of course, and Judge Hogge had mentioned 'Clear and present danger,' but the term had yet to be defined.

There would be no trial this time. After all – a truck loaded with *food*!

'But what,' Scott asked, 'would you offer me as a driver, rather than as Shotgun?'

Taylor pursed his lips, studying the youngster. 'About two hundred a week, for starts.'

Scott nodded. 'Yeah. And a Shotgun you offered three-fifty. You say this is the first rip-off you've taken in six weeks, Mr. Taylor. But I notice you'll pay a kid who's handy with a gun a lot more than a man with a family who drives like he was born in the cab of a truck.'

Taylor didn't answer. He merely sat studying the serious-faced, pale-eyed youth before him. 'Yeah,' he said at last. 'You're a bright one, all right, and I think you'll be moving on after a while. But yes, there's a job here for you. I'm not sure what, right now. What're you good at?'

Scott didn't bother to mention anything farm-oriented. 'I read faster than you can, and I'm very quick with figures.' He tapped his head. 'In my head, I mean.'

Taylor spread his hands again. 'That's what I mean, Scotty. What I need is manual labor – or a Shotgun like you. But what you've got to offer isn't oriented to the trucking business. You're white collar.'

'Yes . . . but I'm only halfway to a degree.'

'Halfway? You mean you're half through college at eighteen?'

Scott looked down, then raised his head with an easy smile, a rather tight grin. 'I just turned seventeen. I lied. I'm not old enough to be paid for gun-toting.'

'Jesus,' Taylor muttered. 'Oh, I guess I'm safe. I'm going to pay you a hundred and seventy-five for that run, Scotty, but it's a *reward*, not a *payment*. That way if someone asks questions, I can't get into trouble. You were just a passenger on that truck.'

'That's right.' Scotty nodded with solemnity and without a hint of twinkle in the icy eyes.

'OK.' Taylor punched a button on his deskcom. 'Paul? Come on in, will you?'

After a moment the driver entered, a big man with a little

too much jowl and gut. His complexion was dark, his forehead very high as his brown hair retreated. He grinned at Scott.

'Paul, Scotty here was a *passenger*, strictly that. He just happened to have a gun and helped out, and I'm going to give him a reward. He's seventeen.'

Paul stared at the boy. 'Jesus,' he said, with feeling.

'Yeah. I not only can't hire him as Shotgun for another year, but he says he doesn't want that kind of job anyhow. He's coming to work here, though.'

Paul looked blank, and Scott's eyes flickered from one man to the other. There wasn't any job, other than Shotgunning. There never were, in cities. He should have known. Taylor was making a job for him. To have him around, to be nice to the kid who'd saved the first truck and maybe a couple of others. *And to have my fast gun and accuracy on the premises.* Scott sighed. And Dad had hardly paid him any attention: it was he and Alex and Andy that were the *men*. Scott was a boy. Second son.

Too bad, he thought, *I can't let Dad know who was the supershot in that first truck. He'll be seeing it on TV, I expect.*

'He needs a place to stay,' Taylor said.

Paul clamped a big red-veined hand on Scott's shoulder. 'I'll take care of that,' he said. 'You stay with me tonight, kid.'

'Scott,' Scott corrected. 'But you've got a run to Cincinnati tomorrow.'

'Aw no. I'm off tomorrow. Don't you think I've earned a couple days?'

'Use them,' Taylor said, 'to find Scotty a place to crash. But two days only, Paul. We did lose a truck today.'

'Insurance?' Scott asked, and Taylor stared at him.

'On a food truck? In the city?' Taylor shook his head. 'Rates're more than the profits on the whole convoy. No, I have to eat that loss, and make up for it with an extra run or two.'

'Come on, Scott,' Paul said, 'let me introduce you to a

couple of people. Then we'll go home and see what Alice's got for supper.'

Scott nodded and went out with Paul, conscious of his employer's eyes on his back.

Chapter Fourteen

Naturally Paul was grabbed by his big blonde wife the moment he entered the apt, and naturally they clinched and Paul swatted her fanny and she clung to him; she'd already heard the news of the demo and had interrupted her supper preparations to watch the early TV coverage. Paul noticed that Scott looked away as they held each other, murmuring and making little exclamations. But it wasn't just that the quiet boy had turned away from embarrassment or politeness; his jaw was clenched. He had something against hugging?

He was not only great with their ten-year-old daughter Mary, he accidentally called her Janie once. And went very dark in the face and was suddenly silent, morose.

He was shocked at their food, although he tried to cover up. He ate a lot, as much as Paul, which made Alice frown.

Reminded of his holstered revolver, he hung it over the back of his chair. He was not accustomed to taking it off, evidently, until reminded . . . by a mother?

He watched with interest the late news coverage of the rip-off of Taylor's food-truck convoy, but he really sat up and leaned forward to watch the special program that followed: on the non-city dwellers. And he seemed to participate in the rip-off of the farm, again clenching his teeth and going stony-faced as he watched.

Paul said nothing. Alice made a bed for the boy on the couch, gave him breakfast in the morning, and he and Paul went out to do a little looking. First they headed for a drugstore to buy Scott a respirator. He looked up every time a jet went over.

'You act like you're not accustomed to planes,' Paul said.

Scott shook his head. 'I'm not. That goes on all the time, doesn't it?'

'Sure. Not where you come from?'

'Nuh-uh. We're not in any flight paths. I just never thought about it. It's still – I mean it was still odd to see a plane, where I came from. Doesn't it drive you nuts?'

'No.' Paul chuckled. 'We'd all be insane if it did.'

'Uh-huh.' Scott nodded thoughtfully. 'I'll bet that's part of it at that, in the cities. Your screens blotted the sound out, right?'

'Most of it,' Paul said. 'Alice really wants one of those resonator things, to set up counter-sound waves or however it works. But they cost money, and we're just not that well off yet. Some apartments come with them, nowadays. But we can't afford one of those, either.' He sighed. 'It costs me a week's pay for the two rooms and bath we've got now, dammit. Seems a guy just never can get ahead.'

'Yeah,' Scott said, watching the people pass, glancing up at the buildings, studying the (almost) sexlessly dressed women. 'I'll bet there's a high incidence of hearing defects, huh?'

Paul laughed. 'You talk mighty fancy for a farmboy who's the fastest gun in the East.'

Scott shrugged. 'Hey – this is a *store*.' The drugstore – which still sold drugs, along with everything else – was a block square. And, as always, packed with people. Paul showed Scott how to slip his wallet into his shirt, above the belt. It was a little uncomfortable, and perhaps not beautiful. But it was a way to make certain it didn't get lifted in the crowd in the store or on the street. People in the cities never carried wallets in wallet pockets, he said.

The girl was young and pretty, and Paul flirted a little and was obviously surprised when Scott didn't. Scott didn't know how.

'Well, if we can't have *that*,' Paul grinned, 'my friend here would like to have a respirator.'

'What size do you wear?' she asked, smiling at Scott. She wore a shapeless sweater that she belted in the store, to make herself a little more attractive than on the street.

That was all he could see; she stood behind the counter. Short hair, little makeup.

Scott shook his head. 'I don't know.'

She looked surprised. 'You don't know what size you wear?'

'He's just in off a farm,' Paul explained.

She directed her wide-eyed gaze to him, then back to Scott. 'Don't you have to wear respirators on farms?' She sounded as if she wouldn't believe he didn't, regardless of what he said.

He shook his head. 'Not on ours, anyhow,' he said, hoping that would help her believe him.

'Well, I'd guess about a. . . .' She put her head on one side, studying him. (He flushed.) 'A nine,' she decided, and found one on the counter, and handed it to him. And looked astonished as Paul had to help him get it on.

'Hey, you're as smart as you are pretty,' Paul smiled. 'This is his size, all right.'

'Well, I've had a lot of experience,' the girl said. 'You know how it is, when you get used to something. You start being able to judge pretty well. Now we have all makes, and—'

'I saw a BreatheFree on TV last night,' Scott said.

'Careful,' Paul told him, eyeing the nearby boy in the ratty clothing. The boy caught his gaze and moved on to try someone else's pocket. 'BreatheFrees don't come cheap.'

'Well,' the girl said, 'it is the best. And there is an inversion warning for tomorrow ni—' Her voice trailed off as she looked past Scott's shoulder, frowning. 'Listen, the guard sure is watching you two.'

When Paul and Scott followed her gaze, the man in the blue uniform looked away. Paul frowned, then nodded.

'It's that gun, Scott. People just don't carry them openly.'

Frowning, the girl put both hands on the plass as she leaned forward to peer over the counter. She pushed herself hurriedly back, her eyes widening. 'My gosh! No wonder – do you always carry that thing?'

Scott nodded.

'Did you see the East Gate demo on TV last night?' Paul asked.

'Sure,' she said, looking from Scott to him and back at Scott, frowning in puzzlement.

'Paul—' Scott said.

'Remember the first truck, the one the caster said got through so handily because of an unidentified young man who was such a deadly shot?'

'Paul—'

'Of course. What's – don't tell me you're the one!'

Scott shot Paul a disgusted gaze, then looked down. 'Yeah.'

'Good grass, you're a hero. The TV people want to talk to you. They said this morning Mr.— whoever the trucker is, I forget – he wouldn't give out your name. Gosh, why not? You're a hero!' Suddenly she glanced at Paul. 'Are you tagging me?'

'No. Seriously. He's the one. He—'

Scott gave him another look, then jerked away from the counter and pushed past a fat couple into the mass of people crowding the store.

'Scott! Hey, Scott!'

The girl came bustling out from behind the counter. 'He's shy, you silly,' she snapped, giving Paul a dark and dark-eyed look. 'Watch this counter. I know your name; your picture was on TV this morning. I remember now.' And she pushed into the throng of customers after Scott.

He had just been shoved violently by a huge man with fiery eyes when the girl came up beside him. She put both hands on Scott's arm. The right one. It was trembling.

'Please excuse him, Mister,' she said to the man, whose fists were doubled up until the knuckles were white. 'We – we just had a little spat.' She smiled at Scott, clinging to him. 'I'm sorry, darling.'

'Better learn not to ram into people, boy,' the man said, and Scott's arm jerked and trembled in the girl's grasp. The man looked down at Scott's hand. The fingers were like a claw, caging the gunbutt thrusting up from his holster. The man's eyes snapped back up to Scott's face and widened still more.

The big man did some jostling of his own as he hurried away.

The girl's fingers were tight on his arm. 'You're dangerous,' she said. 'First, the big rule is: DON'T TOUCH ANYBODY. People can walk and walk all day, in a crowd just like this, and hardly anybody ever touches anyone else. If you do, apologize fast and tell some quick lie to quiet the other person down. You never know what's going to set people off. And then poof – a demo. They pop up over nothing.'

Scott stared at her, studying her face. His arm relaxed. 'I guess I am dangerous,' he said. 'I was ready to pull this thing out and use it, if I had to. He was an arrogant bas – baboon.'

She nodded. 'Bastard too,' she said. 'But you *did* jostle him. Now come on back and let's get a respirator on you. And a pair of glasses, too. Did you know you have eyes like a – a wolf?'

He snorted. 'How would you know what a wolf's eyes look like? There haven't been any wolves for almost twenty years, and you aren't even that old.'

'Well, Mr. Old-Timer, your eyes look like what I *think* a wolf's eyes would look like. Would have, I mean.' She looked into his face again. 'Funny. Now they don't. They're all soft and innocent. You're really a bubbler, aren't you? What's your name?'

They were moving back to her counter, where Paul stood, looking emphatically uncomfortable.

'Sc – oh no. You'll have to swear not to tell anyone,' he said.

'Not to – why not? Don't tell me you're wanted in eighteen states?'

He chuckled. 'No. I just don't want the TV people to know.'

'You really are shy, aren't you? I noticed that right away. I don't think your friend has even found that out yet. Men can be pretty darned dumb, you know? All right.

I give you my solemn word of honor I won't tell the TV people.' She smiled.

'Or anyone else.'

'Or anyone else.'

'I'm Scott Andrews.'

'Hi, Scott Andrews. I'm Nancy Gorman. Have you ever been to Lexington before?'

Scott shook his head. He wouldn't tell her he'd never been to any city, no place bigger than Morehead's 20,000 anyhow. And twenty thousand people constituted a village.

'You embarrassed him,' she told Paul. 'He's shy, silly. He didn't *want* you to tell me about him.' She went efficiently behind the counter. 'Well, there won't be another word about that. You just try on this size nine BreatheFree, Mr. Andrews, and let's see how you look.'

Scott got the mask on, accepting Paul's help with reluctance, and went over to look at himself in the mirrored pillar the girl pointed out. Paul leaned on the counter, grinning at both her and Scott. Scott shook his head and came back to them.

'I look like a monster,' he said. 'An invader from Ceres, at the very least.'

She laughed. 'Well, so does everyone else, then. But it will do the job, and if that inversion thing happens tomorrow the way they predict – you'll be glad you've got it. Good grass, you just aren't *used* to city air, Mr. Andrews.' She looked at Paul. 'I think he'd better take it.'

'It costs too much,' Paul said.

She looked from him to Scott, frowning. 'I'll bet I could get you a job,' she said, 'in about five minutes. Two-seventy-five a week or so.'

Paul winced, Scott frowned over the respirator. 'Doing what?' His voice was hollow, not tinny; the BreatheFree was a good mask.

She waved a hand. 'Guard here,' she said. 'All you have to do is tell them who you are, what you did yesterday, I mean, and—'

'How much for this thing?' he asked, taking it off.

'It's twenty-four ninety-nine, and tax,' she said. 'But—'

Scott reached into his shirt and brought out his wallet. He gave her a twenty and a five, then frowned and added another five. He'd almost forgotten the eight percent sales tax.

She took it, frowning, gazing at his eyes – which would not meet hers – and looking as if she wanted to cry. She turned away, moving slowly and carefully; cash was an unusual commodity.

She turned back with his change, counted it out, then looked at Paul.

'You'd better tell him,' she said, without glancing at Scott, 'that money's not only not accepted at many places, it isn't safe to carry.'

'He just got here yesterday,' Paul said, nonplussed, 'and this is the first place we've been.'

'Well, you'd better get him some glasses, and then go straight to a bank,' she said. She seemed to have resolved not to look at Scott again. If that was the case, she changed her mind. Suddenly she bent a little across the counter toward him, ignoring the short dark woman who had a boxed respirator in one hand and ID card in the other.

'I'm sorry, Scott,' she said. 'I didn't mean to make you mad or hurt you.'

He nodded. The grey-blue eyes were flat, cold.

'You – you are a little touchy,' she said quietly. 'Maybe – pardon me, but maybe you ought to work on that.'

'Yeah,' he said just as quietly, not looking at her. 'I'll try.'

'Scotty, why don't we ask this young lady to—'

'Young woman, are you going to sell me this mask or not?'

Nancy glanced at the customer, back at Paul and Scott, and bit her lip. Then she took the woman's card to make the credit transfer, and of course when she turned back the man and the fair-haired youth were gone.

'She liked you, Scott. You struck up a friendship, just like that, and she was a doll. We could have asked her to lunch, or something. If you're going to blow your money on expensive masks like that, you might as well blow a little on a pretty girl.' Paul's hand clamped his shoulder.

Scott looked oddly at him, blinking, obviously considering.

'Really? Is that all it takes? For a girl, I mean.'

It was Paul's turn to frown. 'Sure. Really. God, you act like you've lived in Outer Mongolia all your life. Aren't there any girls where you come from?'

Again Scott's face went dark – it was the only way to describe the cloud, the shadow that seemed to descend over it. As if a curtain had fallen, or Scott had somehow pulled drapes between him and the world.

'Here,' Paul said, 'try these blue ones and take a peek at yourself in a mirror.'

Scott did, bought the blue glasses, and they went out of the store and down the street to the First National Bank and Trust Company. Scott's deposit was very small; a hundred and forty one dollars might get him a room for a month somewhere, provided he didn't eat until he got some more money. Paul offered; Scott refused.

'Listen,' Scott said as they emerged from the bank into the fastmoving throng of the Downtown Island, 'if we should happen to get separated or something, just don't worry about it. I know how to get to your place, and I'll be there for supper.' He smiled. 'If I'm welcome, I mean.'

'Of course,' Paul said, grinning. 'But let's don't get separated. The crowd isn't *that* bad. We'll just hang close, buddy. OK? think we ought to go back to the warehouse and see if somebody there needs a roommate or knows about an apartment.'

Scott nodded, but at ten minutes to twelve Paul lost him.

Chapter Fifteen

'Why yes,' Nancy told him, 'I'd be delighted to have lunch with you, Mr. Andrews.'

'Scott,' he said.

'Scott,' she nodded. 'I get off in twenty minutes, for two

hours. I had a choice when I took the job: either two days a week off and an hour for lunch, or one day and two hours for lunch. Well, girls just never seem to have long enough lunch hours. So.' She shrugged smiling.

'How many hours a day do you work?'

'I come in at ten and go to lunch at 12:30, and come back at 2:30. Then I work till 5:30. Four days a week.' She shrugged. 'Just a job.'

He nodded, thinking about it as he wandered around the drugstore, waiting for the recalcitrant hand on the clock to jerk, one minute at a time, down to 12:30.

She worked twenty two hours a week. Paul worked two days, then was off two days. Anything else was overtime, extra money. That way more people got to work less time, and as long as prices were high enough, everyone could live on that basis. Or something like that; economics was one thing Scott hadn't gone into too deeply, and didn't intend to. At home there were Jeff and Josie, Alex and Deb, and Andy, Kristy, Roger, and . . . Scott. Theirs wasn't a commercial farm, by any means. They fed themselves, and bought things; his father had income both from royalties and from current novels, although so few people seemed to read nowadays that his advances had failed to rise in accord with the cost of living.

But they kept busy. There was always work to be done. Weeding, that was the worst. Picking off beetles or bugs or worms. Digging potatoes, picking and then shelling peas, pulling onions and carrots and defoliating and washing them; on and on. Gathering walnuts and letting them dry awhile, then husking off the yellow outer shells until your hands were brown up to here, a brown that would come off only with time: wear. Then there were the women-things like canning and preserving, which were the same but which Josie separated, vocally. On and on.

He knew that people with commercial farms worked a lot more. Many hours daily, many hours weekly, *every* day. And four- and five-people farms still produced over half the country's food as they always had; the pair-territory of papa and mama and maybe a hired man in addition to the children. Take two days off from feeding the chickens? Work a four-hour day when cows had to be milked twice daily? He smiled, wandering through the store – and he was stared at.

He wondered: what would happen to the country if people on farms tried working like people in the cities? What would happen if there ever came a time when *all* the children left the farms? For years they had been leaving, drawn mothlike to the city's lights and glamor and the prospects of big factory money – at regular hours, and extra money for working overtime, because pressure was the boss's problem, not the laborer's.

There wouldn't be any country, he decided. None at all. We'd all starve, and quickly. The big commercial farms with all their workers and machinery still produce less per man-hour per acre than the little mom-and-pop farms of less than 500, often less than 300 acres. Because of ownership. Because of territory, his father had told him, and had written, at length, in his last non-fiction book, *Quo In Arco Vadimus?*. People worked for themselves, always, harder and with more enthusiasm and, consequently, production, than when they worked for someone else – on someone else's property.

Just as the man with the tiny house almost invariably kept it in better condition than the man who rented one, or even who rented a furnished house.

That wasn't to say that people didn't work when they were employees, or let their apts go to hell. But whether in farm or factory or – or in writing, Jeff Andrews had pointed out, reminding them of his hours at the typewriter, which was work, even if it *was* his hobby – or in keeping up a dwelling, people put out more effort when it was *their* store, *their* farm, *their* house, *their* typewriter (as opposed, say, to that of a newspaper). And their Thing, Scott's father said. Which was why he had never accepted an assignment. He'd been afraid to. He had one hell of a time writing anything other than his Thing, from his mind.

Everyone could not be self-employed; the concept was ridiculous. Not everyone wanted to be, or was capable of being. The failure of so many men to make it in the insurance business – back in the days when the companies' objective was to get everyone to buy as much life insurance as possible – was due in great part to their inability to manage themselves. Some had that built-in ignition switch and the self-control necessary for self-management. Most didn't. His father called writing his hobby. He had never seemed to grow accustomed to the fact, to accept the fact, that he was making a living by engaging in his hobby. Still, he handled it as a business, and Scott knew he had forced himself to sit in front of that typewriter on days when he'd rather have done something else, on days when the words did not seem to come. But Jeff Andrews had done it, for years, and he had shaken his head over those others who wanted to be writers but who did not want to write, and those who wanted to write but who just could not exercise the necessary self-discipline.

That was self-employment. It offered both positive and negative adjuncts, and some people, probably most, just couldn't handle the negatives.

Scott supposed ownership of property was pretty much the same, although he knew that his kind – like most other members of the animal kingdom, including fish and birds – had a need to own, to possess.

He looked around.

You can force people to give up all their possessions and become part of an anthill gestalt, his father had said, by applying the iron heel to the neck. By totalitarianism. Or you can force them via the pressures of population and industrialization, crowding and specialization and cybernation. In the first group, you have a bunch of heel-dragging, drooping-chinned cattle, until some day Comes the Revolution. In the second case, if you try maintaining the pretense of freedom, of government by *res-publicae* or *demos-kratos*, you have little revolutions on a daily basis.

'You have our cities,' Scott muttered, and the little woman beside him jerked violently, staring. She scuttled away horrified. Not, he thought, because he had slipped up and talked to himself. She was horrified that he might have been talking to her.

He stopped at the Old Days display to examine the white polyethylene masks with their washable filters. Beside the mask was a copy of the old ad. It showed the heads of a man and a woman, looking happy with the masks covering their mouths and noses. ALL-PURPOSE MASK AND FILTERS, the headline read, and 'Are you allergic to household dust or paint sprays . . . pollen in late summer?' And so on. The masks were a dollar ninety-eight, a packet of extra filters sixty-five cents. People paused to examine the '70's ad, to chuckle both at the unimportant reasons for masking and at the price.

People had tried to wear those during the killer temperature-air inversions that had slain so many during the seventies and early eighties, he knew. And their deaths were the more pitiful for their having thought they were safe, behind their silly little masks. Those were the days when people died in the streets, died outside hospital emergency rooms and on hospital steps, because there was no way to crowd anyone else into hallways already packed with panting, wheezing, gasping, eye-bulging citizens of all ages. Conveniently, for militant youth, those ever more frequent days and nights of horror had killed far more old persons than young.

Then the factory burnings and bombings had become more frequent than the inversion horrors. Eventually most of Detroit had gone. Fires had a way of spreading. Firemen had a way of being killed, one way or another.

Scott jumped a little as a hand touched his arm. He swung, going tight, to find Nancy there, smiling, explaining that it was 12:35 and she'd been looking for him in the store for five minutes. They went out to eat, fighting the crowds that made the downtown island almost safe.

'A crowd can always explode into a demo at the slightest excuse,' the girl told him, 'but generally speaking it's safer to be surrounded by people than alone. With people all around something *might* happen. If you're alone, though, you can bet that something *will* happen.'

By the time they finished lunch he had learned to be a little more comfortable with a girl, with another person, and he had learned to relax a little as he learned more about city life. And he had learned that Nancy was eighteen, and shared an apt with another girl a year older, and he had a date for that evening. A real date, a real old-fashioned girl-boy rendezvous.

MEANWHILE: VIII

A City Is A Helluva Place To Live, But It's A Great Place For Dying

Danny and Mose had mugged the old lady and got a credit card and some other stuff, and they had grabbed a couple dumb enough to try to park for a little necking. They beat hell out of the punk and both of them ripped the girl's clothes mostly off and gave her a damned good sinking. It was good stuff.

Chucko and Keys and Horseprick had jumped the car at the light without stopping to question why it was the only car there at that time of night. Guy and his wife. Chucko just leaned on the hood, with his little one-twenty-five laser leveled straight at the wide-eyed woman staring at him through the windshield, while Keys stood beside her door and Horse beside her husband's. Helplessly the guy opened up, of course, but he had come out with an old .32 in his white fist and Horse had to give him a knee in the rocks before providing him with a second belly-button with the knife. Horse had wanted to take time out to sink that bludgeon between his legs into the guy's wife, who was not screaming, just making chicken noises and crying, but Chucko and Keys had managed to get him into the car and the woman out. It brought a pretty good piece of change at Dilly's. On the way back, spoiling for a fight, they had tangled with a pair of baboons from the Transy area, the ghetto formed by the old buildings of the (former) college. They had gutted one and howled with laughter as the other one ran off, yelling, with three fingers on his right hand busted.

Turko and the new bird Berto had busted up a little pot party down under the Viaduct and beat hell out of one of the punks. The other one, along with one of the girls, ran off. The second chick was so good-looking and had such an unbelievable shape they'd brought her back with them.

The girl gasped in pain and shocked astonishment when they showed her the old-fashioned hypodermic needle, the kind they used to use to shoot anesthetic or antibiotic or whatever kind of juice it was straight into the vein. Anyhow. Vic showed her what a funthing it was to have that long skinny needle rammed into a hindcheek, and she squealed and jumped, and then did a lot more squealing and gasping and groaning and panting as Vic and Horse and Hogjaw played with her. Her throat hurled out shrieks till they knew it ached like raw burger. Her mouth dribbled moans. She grunted in pain, thrashing helplessly beneath Horse while Vic continued playing with her, using the hypo on her jugs. Horse grunted and shivered and then pulled out with a sound like dragging a foot out of clutching mud, and Vic piled on and in. She wasn't squealing or anything like that anymore, now. A little sound of exhaustion, of conquered submission trembled from her slack mouth. She was nearly still, conquered, soft and naked and shamefully, obscenely open and accessible. She lay in dazed submissiveness, in helpless defeat and acceptance of whatever came next. Vic came next. Then Chucko.

Shanks turned up his nose at her, so the new bird Berto did, too. He usually did whatever Shanks did. So they opened the door and slung her in with the other girls. Most of them got so they liked it. What the hell, they got fed, they got plenty of sex, and they didn't have to worry about a thing.

'Berto baby,' Shanks said as they enjoyed a joint in relative silence, lying up fat and sassy after a pretty good night's take, 'your old apt's having a big party tonight. All floors in the Common Room. Berto, we are going to rip off your old man's apt tonight. Sweet revenge.'

Bert's eyes went wide. 'Aw no, Shanks, naw, naw. Don't make me do that. Sure I hate the old bastard, but . . . naw, I won't do it.'

So Shanks had Chucko and Vic grabbed the punky new bird, and Horse pulled out his big knife and peeled open

Berto's shirt and set the point against Berto's navel and started leaning on it.

'Your chief wants your help, Bert-Ross boy,' Horse said, sneering the silly name. 'And you better give it to him, too, unless you want an extra belly-button.'

And pretty soon Berto agreed.

But when they got there they found that all the locks and codes had been changed. Berto was no help at all in getting them into the building. Then Shanks forced him to call his apt, by which time Berto was sobbing. But there was no answer. His parents and the sister Helen he'd mentioned were either at the big apt-party or out. Shame; Shanks had been saving his juice for that little sinkbait.

Angry and disappointed, Shanks and his boys, the Woodlawn Hawks, made a lot of ugly noises and milled around in the lot behind the building. Then they decided to just hang around and wait awhile until someone came home and maybe they could get in that way. They'd wait an hour, Shanks said. It was one-twenty a.m.

Chapter Sixteen

Scott called Paul and told him he had a date and would be eating with Nancy; Paul was delighted. Scott kidded with him a little, saying he was just pleased because he – Scott – ate so much. Sure, he'd noticed how they watched. He was sorry; he was used to meat. Paul told him not to do anything he wouldn't do and they switched off.

Scott spent the afternoon wandering in and out of stores in the Downtown Island. The city was fascinating. The stores were fascinating. But the people were the most interesting of all. Scott watched them, listened to them, observed their habits and rites, and began thinking maybe Dad was right. Maybe he *could* write, particularly now that he knew a little more, now that he'd seen a little more. Now that he'd seen a city and seen how its inmates looked and behaved.

Touching was hard to avoid, but they performed admirably, astonishingly well at avoiding body contact. They spoke to each other even less than they touched, Scott noticed. People spoke to people only when one was a clerk and the other a customer, or when they were berating each other for some minor transgression, such as jostling, or when they were obviously previously acquainted.

Strangers, Scott noticed, just didn't speak, and he amused himself by saying things to people and noting their reactions. They were varied, but all were familiar. They were surprised, and a little rankled, ready to turn hot words on someone so gauche as to break their code and speak to someone he obviously did not know. (By this time he had bought a pair of trousers and no longer wore the jeans. But he wore his gun, of course.) Nearly everybody was armed, but most had their weapons concealed in a purse or pocket or sleeve.

He sat down and asked for a cup of coffee, but was advised with a chuckle that there wasn't any coffee. No, no tea either; you been living in a cave, kid? So he settled for a Coke, with imitation cherry flavoring it. All was made out of chemicals. He watched the people around him by looking across the counter at the mirror. He considered.

Had they become a *noyau*, a society held together only by mutual antipathy, after all these years as one of the most fiercely territorial-patriotic countries on the planet? He wondered. There was no way to know, of course, unless someone attacked, openly, an American installation somewhere. Nationalizing American industry overseas or knocking off a few American nationals here and there in other countries and raping their women . . . those didn't count. People didn't identify with those, didn't consider that an attack on the country. Despite overseas military divisions here and there, masquerading as 'UN,' an abstract term that had achieved no more solidity than solidarity, there would be no more Vietnams. Not after the wave of legislation, years ago, that had tied the president's hands tightly and left him as just what he'd been intended, once George Washington's friends had got over his refusal to be called

'Your Majesty' or the other titles they suggested and he rejected. The president was now what he was before Jackson and Teddy Roosevelt and then, in quick succession. Truman-Kennedy-Johnson, had broadened his powers because he was called Commander-in-Chief.

Now he was Chief Executive again, and Tonkin was a filthy word. Rather like a corporate president, an employee of a strong board of directors. His directors in the Senate and on the Hill accepted most of his suggestions and recommendations, unless party differences got in the way. But they made the final decisions. The president was . . . an executive. A corporate president. These days, of course, people feared the Senate (and HEW), not the president, and used words such as 'oligarchy.'

But have we become a *noyau*, Scott Andrews wondered, watching his fellow man in the counter-mirror of Walgreen's on Main near Limestone.

He couldn't be sure. He was very very bright, and he knew it. Just as his father had known far more by eighteen than his own father had by fifty, because of the communications that exploded right along with the population, Scott's education and store of information and, more importantly, *understanding* far exceeded his father's when Jeff Andrews had been thirty or so. But Scott knew what a *noyau* was, and he wondered. He decided that it was probably only a temporary manifestation. The country could become that, in time – unless something such as Pearl Harbor happened again. Then the collection of strangers masquerading as a nation would in all likelihood reassume the ancient snarl turned by territorial proprietors against threatening intruders, and start smiling at each other again. While they beat the hell out of the intruder.

Would it really take that, Scott Andrews wondered. *And – would it be worth it? Is involvement in a 'just' war – ignoring the contradiction in terms – really the only thing that pulls man together?*

He wasn't sure if he wanted to know or not.

At 5:30 he went back to the enormous drugstore to meet Nancy, now far less feminine in her loosely unbelted street clothes. He and she, with a neighbor couple, walked down the street to join the crowd waiting for the big double-decker electric buses. Slowly they moved forward, ever pressing and being pressed from behind toward the curb, watching bus after bus move up, ingest humanity in front and disgorge it from the rear, and move off again in a continuous stream of huge yellow vehicles like little houses on wheels. Within fifteen minutes they were aboard one, Nancy treating him to the ride by flashing her monthly pass and saying 'Guest', and climbing to the second level because she and her friends wanted Scott to see the street from up here.

The bus was strictly an out-island express, meaning it made one stop at one downtown corner and then drove steadily until it was out of the island and into residential areas, stopping at every other corner.

After the third stop they were all able to sit down, with Scott over next to the window. He gazed out with high interest, trying to fill his mind with it. He heard only the sounds of the air conditioner and passengers, of course; buses were sealed, like all other vehicles and most buildings, against the ear-destroying, sanity-attacking outside noises.

The other couple lived in the same apartment building as Nancy, and they all walked down the street together, with Nancy and Scott behind Bill and whatever her name was, his wife. Nancy nodded at the passing armored car, explaining that it was a grocery delivery truck.

'Why doesn't it say so?' Scott asked, with the sweet innocence of a bonafide card-carrying hick.

Nancy shot him a look. 'A truck carrying *food? You* should know! Good grass! It doesn't pay to advertise, you know!'

A couple of tough-looking males eyed them as they walked toward them, and one of them called something to Bill's wife, grinning. Scott noticed that his companions ignored the pair. Scott didn't, although he pretended to. (After a few moments he realized that that was exactly what his companions were doing, staring straight ahead and keepinp a peripherally viewing eye on the toughs. 'Baboons', they called them in cities.) Scott wasn't going to step aside for them, but Nancy grasped his wrist and yanked. He stumbled against her. The baboons sauntered by, chuckling.

He looked at her.

'Yes,' she said, gazing into his eyes, 'you probably could have. But why? One tries to avoid trouble, Scott. You seem to look for it.'

He thought about that, chewing his lip and squinting, and he was still thinking about it when they reached the soaring building and paused while Bill gave the codes, then used his key. They all went in and got on the elevator. Bill and his wife got off, with goodbyes, on Three. Nancy and Scott went on up to Seventeen. And along the hall, and Nancy paused before a door to speak her codes into the grille before keying it open.

Inside Scott met Nancy's roommate-aptsister Peggy. She was Scott's height and close to his build; slim, with short, wavy blonde hair and eyes so dark he knew the hair was dyed. Two-thirds of the people in cities, he had read, dyed their hair now, including over thirty-seven percent of the males. It was one way to be an individual. Another way was to dress the way you pleased in your own apt, where you didn't have to worry about being eyed – and what might follow being eyed.

Peggy wore a bright red jumper whose straps crossed between her naked breasts – bumps with overdeveloped aureoles, nothing more – and whose skirt cleared the bottom of her bottom by about one centimeter. And thigh boots, also red and shiny-wet-plastic (dearhyde; the deer-skin people had lost the suit) with side press-closures all the way down.

She was nineteen, with the underdeveloped figure of an eleven- or twelve-year-old (Scott hadn't seen his sister Kristy's chest for years, but he was sure it had bigger bumps) – and the sensual manner and poise of a thirty-year-old courtesan.

'This,' she said, 'is about the handsomest but also the

oddest thing you've ever brought home, Nance, Lord, Scott Andrews, you've got enough freckles for three other people. Got em all over?'

Scott flushed, and Peggy stared, then turned her startled eyes on Nancy. 'My gawd. He blushes. Can I have him? I haven't met a male who blushed since I was eleven and cherry.'

Nancy chuckled, taking Scott's arm in both hands. 'Easy, easy, Peg. He's from out of town, and he's a little shy, and about twice as smart as anybody you ever met. He's also – can I tell her, Scott?'

Of course she could; things were different now. Scott felt that the girl who managed to be simultaneously stringy and supersexy had laughed at him, put him down. He nodded. Nancy squeezed his arm.

'He also doesn't carry that thing on his hip to keep his thigh warm,' she told Peggy, whose eyes dropped to the holster. 'This is the guy the News called the "unidentified sharpshooter", who brought that first food truck right through the East Gate yesterday; remember the TV thing? The East Gate demo?'

Peggy folded her arms under her breasts, or rather under each half of her chest, its center clearly marked by bone-structure. She stared at him. 'No.'

'Yes.'

She still stared, waiting for Scott to corroborate. He nodded, looking away. Despite wanting to impress her, he just couldn't look at her full on.

'Dear god,' Peggy said, 'you're a sinking hero! Sit down, take off your shoes, and let me make us all a drink while Nancy gets out of her work-clothes.'

Scott sat down. The apt seemed to consist of this room with its couch and three chairs in a space about the size of his mother's kitchen, and then, separated by having carpet tiles of a different color and by the little room-divider, a kitchen area about the size of the upstairs bathroom in his father's hilltop home. Nancy smiled at him and went through a doorway and closed it behind her. Bedroom, he thought, wondering where Peggy's was, and where the bathroom was. (There was only one bedroom, of course.)

He glanced over at Nancy, who was bringing a couple of bottles out of a cabinet beneath the sink. His eyes went wide and he stared. He wanted to rip his gaze away from the round buttocks that her black briefs only pretended to cover. But he couldn't.

My God. I'm a provincial ass, he thought, thinking of home, and his mother, and Deb, and Kristy, and the girl they'd captured two months ago after that big rip attempt, and how Dad had had to have a talk with her about the way they dressed in the house, and how he had heard her with Andy once and seen her with him another time and then seen them the third time, in the trees, thrashing about in the leaves. She'd been a captive of the rippers, and she was from Ashland, which Dad had established with a couple of phone calls. Then he established her intelligence. After that he ignored hers and Andy's mutual attraction. Within a week Suzanne was certain she didn't want to go back to Ashland, which after all was a city, even though it was only a hundred thousand or so, part of a much larger tri-city/tri-state complex formed by Ashland Kentucky and Ironton Ohio and Huntington West Virginia. Within five weeks Suzanne and Andy had been a Thing, with her taking great pleasure in ignoring Scott and Andy's assuming a bristling-threatening male attitude toward him, and Scott took it all he could, unable to think about anything but girls, all day and all night. Then he'd left, with a wild and quarter-assed notion of kidnapping himself a wife.

And now he sat and stared at Nancy's aptsister's completely exposed and only partially covered rump, and his stomach twisted up and over and his throat was dry and his new trousers were suddenly too tight.

About that time she turned to look back at him, grinning. He knew it was deliberate, her bending over and displaying herself to him this way. She pretended not even to notice or be aware.

'Do you like martinis?'

Scott had last tasted a martini when he was twelve. He'd

made a face and drunk a glass of Kool-aid immediately.

'Ah – no,' he said, thinking desperately. He had to say something; he was already a self-pronounced bumpkin. The others she and Nancy brought home probably hadn't paid a bit of attention to things like the bare little lumps of Peggy's chest, adorned with their emphatically swollen and deeply pink tips, or to her – rump, either. And he was obviously expected to drink, no matter what things were like at home.

He named one of his father's favourites: 'Bourbon? With some soda or water and a little lemon?'

She nodded, not looking surprised, and straightened up to mix the drinks. He peeled his gaze from her back and moved it around the room.

The walls were carpeted, alternately, with red and burnt orange. The floor was carpeted with red; the ceiling with burnt orange. Two of the cupchairs were yellow, a sort of gold-orange-yellow, rather than canary, and the third chair was starkly white. The couch was black. The pictures on the walls were wild and colorful, three of them resembling abstract jigsaw puzzles cut by an alcoholic with the DTs, another all white with a red splotch in its center, like a large drop of blood that had fallen from a considerable height. The ZEUS BLESS THIS CAGE sign was black-edged white letters on an orange day-glo background.

There was an electric blue pillow on the couch, and a lavender, and a jonquil-yellow, and a black. And a fat black plastic cushion on the floor against the wall; it could be used for sitting, he saw. (He *had*, after all, seen magazines and TV. It was hardly possible these days even for a provincial to be as *provençal* as in previous years. There were TV, and viewphones – although come to think the Andrewses didn't have one – and of course journals. His father received a half-dozen journals or worse a month, as well as about that many books. A fellow could be a bumpkin, Scott decided, but he didn't have to be an utter idiot.)

'Who did the artwork?' he asked, without looking around at Peggy. He was afraid to.

She laughed. 'Guy I lived with for seven or eight months, last year,' she told him. 'Those snaky ones are my sole legacy from him, unless you count the mis-see.'

He had to think a moment to realize what she meant, and he wondered how she'd been dumb enough to live with some guy for seven or eight months and turn up pregnant. Why hadn't she taken her shots? It all happened so fast his mind seemed to assimilate it without staggering. Click, and he stored that one away. It was OK to talk about having lived with someone of the other sex. And aborting.

Then it occurred to him that he couldn't be sure; Peggy seemed pretty far out. He'd have to try to find out how that fitted in with their code.

Meanwhile the door was opening and Nancy was returning and Scott stood, because he'd been taught to, and the girl coming in only vaguely resembled the girl he'd met today and spent two hours with at lunch and nearly an hour and a half escorting home (about a mile and a tenth, she had told him, although she didn't think in terms of miles; no one in cities did).

He'd met and brought home Nancy 1; this was Nancy 2.

Nancy One had short dark hair, curled interestingly around her ears; Nancy Two's long blonde hair streamed down straight and shiny, in several shades, past her shoulders. Nancy One hadn't appeared completely shapeless in the store, with her smock belted, but her shape hadn't been worth studying or reflecting upon. Nancy Two had a bosom that shot out and swooped down and out and rounded sharply back, and a waist that tucked way in and then flared out in a rush into very female hips that rushed down into round thighs and shapely, if slender, calves. Nancy One had OK eyes and a mouth-mouth and OK eyebrows; Nancy Two's eyes were somehow huge, set in dark almond shapes, and her mouth was full and sensuous and pale purple, and her brows were thick and dark in the current city fashion. She wore a black-and-white harlequin-patterned thing that covered her right breast thoroughly while baring two thirds of the left one, and nearly her right hip while hugging and covering the left one completely. It had been cut out in the heart-shape over the navel, which he could see through a strip of transparent something; plastic, he supposed, but soft, not hard. Her right arm was covered to the wrist; her left bare from above the shoulder. Her legs were encased in something black that was better than nudity, all shiny and unwrinkled and gleaming nearly white at every stress-point, even the backs of her slim calves. Her skirt was a little longer than Peggy's.

Catching his breath and swallowing, trying to pretend he had preserved his aplomb, Scott said, 'I'm Scott Andrews. I don't believe we've met.'

She laughed and skipped to him and hugged him so that he was very aware of the pressures of her breasts and her thighs. She bounced and jiggled and joggled delightfully. She squeezed him hard, giggling, then let go and swung to take the tall glass from Peggy and present it to him. She picked up her martini. Then they sat down to drink and talk.

'Joe is coming?' Nancy asked, her thick brows raised in Peggy's direction. Nancy sat beside Scott on the couch, while Peggy faced them in the white chair with her long legs crossed. (Scott wished Nancy were there, where he could see her better. She was more beautiful, more *female* than anything he had ever seen in magazines or on TV.)

Peggy nodded. 'Joe'll be here about eight,' she said. 'There's an apt-party tonight.'

'Let's skip it.'

Peggy nodded.

They sat and drank and talked – Scott handled the bourbon-and-water-with-lemon carefully, drinking slowly, and found it wasn't too bad, once one got accustomed to the taste of bourbon, and the little burning feeling. He remembered that his father had said he'd got his start drinking sweet stuff, like most people, before he grew up and graduated to enjoying the taste of liquor. He was careful which brands he served to people who drank it with cola or things like 7-up; he never wasted the better bourbon on them. Scott had asked for his father's current preference, not wanting to be juvenile by requesting something sweet.

After all, the two girls were drinking martinis, which as he remembered tasted mostly like hair tonic and perfume.

He had never been so aware of himself. He had never been so aware of the people around him. He had never had such a hard time thinking. He had never had a bad case of the tight pants for so long at one stretch. And certainly he had never been so uncomfortable, and certainly he had never enjoyed himself so much.

'Boy I just wish somebody would break in tonight and try something,' Peggy said, as she and Nancy worked on dinner. 'I'd like to see our freckled hero do his thing!'

'Hush, Peggy, he's *sensitive* about it.'

'Ha! Not after that drink I fixed. How many'd you knock off, Scotty the Kid?'

'Eighty or ninety,' Scott said, being as ridiculous as possible because he knew she wouldn't believe five shots and five shirt-fronts blossoming into bright red flowers that bloomed swiftly and then wilted as their wearers sagged or jerked backward to fall. And he wasn't sure; there might have been six. That one behind the second one had looked as though the bullet might have gone through and into him, but Scott wasn't certain. He'd put in more shooting-time with Alex than with his father, and Alex had taught him his method: shoot and go on to the next target; don't stop to see what you accomplished. Alex had pointed out to him that baseball players did the same thing. A batter hit and ran without taking time to sling the bat or watch the ball. Scott had merely aimed and fired, and was already moving his hand and aiming and firing again as the first scarlet flower started to open.

Thinking about it, he shuddered. God, what he'd done. What a horrible, barbaric, monstrous thing!

And what dark horror was it inside the race of man that he gained such a thrill from his more barbarous activities?

And, he realized, that so thrilled the females of his species. Scotty the Kid, Peggy had called him, and he was suddenly certain that Billy the Kid probably drilled as many hymens as men, the only difference being that the men had lain down after he fired his gun. The fascination with war heroes . . . with murderers, the more monstrous their crimes the better . . . the letters and proposals that accused murderers received from females – and the *stacks* of such letters they received after their convictions! The naked ape had reached his dominion by using his brain, but he still loved to use his brawn and his weapons, and women still grooved far more on muscle and weaponeers than on males with brains. It was Jeff Andrews who had written first that article, then the novel, based on the sexual power and accomplishments of football players as opposed to Phi Beta Kappas. He had even learned that the one football player he'd discovered who was also Phi Beta Kappa had *apparently* been less sexually attractive than his teammates.

Scott thought about that, and about Nancy's first reaction to him, and Peggy's, and he felt a huge growing sense of power and importance. It was the sort of feeling that had assailed millions of other males before him, had enwrapped them and held them in its claws until their deaths, more often premature than not, after lives of being pursued by members of both sexes for entirely different reasons.

Because mama-to-be wants to make sure her womb gets the bestest seed they is, he thought suddenly, without evoking the thought, *and the ancient instincts base that on physical prowess, and weapons-using is considered more an extension of physical prowess than mental. Survival of the fittest . . . but why, then, do we consider killers the fittest, rather than geniuses? Why did they lie down for John Dillinger and Broadway Joe, and not for Fermi and Einstein and every other Nobel winner?*

And then he though maybe he had it, or a line on it. The point was, some females *had* lain down, figuratively or literally, for those, and certainly for artists of all types. (Although that may have been the fascination for showbiz types, what Doctor Schulzinger called the Groupie Syndrome.) Those women had probably been the best breedstock, to be sickeningly scientific about it. A girl who was horrified and sickened by Scott Andrews' ability with a gun, Scott Andrews thought sickly, but is excited and made a little wet by Scott Andrews' brain – she's the best choice for the human race's future.

Not Peggy or Nancy . . . .

Maybe I am a genius, for godssake, Scott thought. *And yes, I think I'll try to write about it. Leaving home and coming down here was the best thing I could have done; in two days, just two days I already know so much more! It's as if my brain had opened all its windows and doors and all sorts of new and fresh and unpolluted air were rushing in!*

'Why are you so silent, Scotty the Kid?' Peggy asked. 'You want another drink? Be about ten minutes yet.'

'E,' Scott said, gazing at her to gauge the effect, 'equals em-see-squared.'

She looked at him as if he were insane.

Chapter Seventeen

Without being ridiculous or obnoxious, without totally losing his head, Scott Andrews made very certain during dinner that both Peggy and Nancy became aware that he had a brain, and that that brain was well-oiled, well-greased, and fueled to overflowing.

He saw that it interested and impressed them, his fine mind and storehouse of knowledge, because he was the second son of a strong man and the first son was also strong and Scott had read and read and engaged in introspection until he was certain he'd exceed his father's present maturity level by the time he was twenty. But he noticed, too, that it made them a bit uncomfortable. They preferred hearing about the big attempted rip at the farm two months ago, and about the trip down here in the food truck. And particularly about the activities at the East Gate.

Someone came to the door, and they went through the ritual of identification before opening it to a shortish, plumpish – or perhaps just well-rounded was the better term – girl Nancy called Helen. She possessed a headful of rather black hair and very pretty legs, (Scott's appreciation of and preference for legs stemmed from his father's preference and his mother's development; he liked big calves) and extraordinarily bright, clear, blue eyes. And a taut blouse.

'You two aren't going down to the apt party?'

'No,' Nancy told her. 'I've got company, and Joe's coming, and I think we'll just stay up here.'

'Oh – excuse me,' the girl said, glancing past Nancy at Scott, who was gazing at her from the couch. She smiled, slightly.

Nancy stepped back and aside. 'Helen, this is Scott Andrews, who is from out of town. Scott, this is Helen Caudill. She and her parents live down the hall.'

'Scott,' Peggy said with as much pride as if he'd been her property for the evening, 'is the sharpshooter who got that first food truck in when the big rip-off try started – and was probably responsible for a lot of the other food that got in.' She glanced at Scott. 'Helen,' she said, in an entirely different tone of voice, 'is a brain. She's got a Hahvahd scholarship.'

Scott stood, which made six female eyebrows rise, because it wasn't the way of the city. 'Recycle,' he said.

'Hi,' Helen said quietly, with a little frown that she turned quickly into a smile just as small. 'I'm – glad to meet you. Thanks for the food.' She returned her attention to Nancy. 'Well, if you're not coming to the party, I wish you'd do me a favor. Mother and Dad are out with the Frasers, and they won't be in until pretty late, I think. You know what it's like when there's an apt party; old Mr. Bowen will be there, wearing his uniform and looking important. That means he'll seal the out-door, and someone will have to let Mother and Dad in. Can I hook up our com to yours?'

'Sure. Want us to call you when they get here?'

'Yes, thanks, and just let them in, all right?'

'Sure, Helen.'

'Thanks.' Helen's eyes swerved to Scott, passed quickly. 'I'm glad to have met you,' she said, and departed.

She looked pretty darned good in the fanny department too, Scott thought. But she sure wasn't turned on by heroes.

Peggy said something snotty about Helen's being a brain, and Nancy hushed her and told Scott about Helen's brother Bert-Ross, who had gone out one night, mad, and hadn't come back. They didn't know if he was dead or not.

'What do they do at apt parties?' Scott asked.

'Oh it's kind of fun,' Nancy told him (Peggy sneered), 'but it gets to be a skid after a while. I mean it's a nice way for everyone to sort of turn loose and get to meet everyone – you saw how Helen was dressed, you sure don't see HER looking that good very often. But the trouble is *everybody's* there. Parents and singles from age twenty to seventy. That kind of electrostatics, you know. You can't really have a lot of fun and be at ease when all those old people are around, gabbing and watching and wishing they were young.'

'And being scandalized by everything you wear and do,' Peggy said. 'Let's get this stuff cleaned up. Joe'll be here in a few minutes.'

They cleaned up, and Joe arrived, wearing one of those strange city haircuts, close-trimmed and almost without sideburns, and a drooping mustache. He wore some sort of shiny blue coverall with a self-belt, and was all grinning and sure of himself, and Scott began to feel pretty bumpkinish again. But Joe greeted him affably enough. He too was impressed, and Scott had to tell the story again. This time Peggy and Nancy interrupted constantly, telling about half of it. With their help the story grew a little.

Nancy turned the rheostat and pushed the button inside it, and the place went dim and blue, and Joe hauled out the present he'd brought, which the girls greeted with squealing delight. Scott considered refusing or making up an excuse to leave, then determined to stay and experience this, too. He wouldn't let them think what they so egoistically called non-city dwellers were all hicks and conservative prigs.

So he too lit a brown tube, and watched them carefully, holding the sweetish smoke in the same way they did after sucking hard the way they did, and it had absolutely no effect on him whatever.

Peggy came over to peer into his eyes. 'Nothing. First-timer?' She moved languidly; she spoke languidly.

Scott admitted it.

She sighed, pushing herself erect by placing her hands on his chest and shoving. She turned to Joe.

'First-timer,' she said. 'Better give him another cup.'

Joe studied Scott through the dim blue haze. At least it seemed a haze, with the rather cloying smoke and smell of the marihuana eddying about in the small, blue-lit room.

'Sure faked well,' he said. 'Thought you'd been igniting for years.'

Scott smiled.

'OK,' Joe said. 'No poppy-parters,' and they gathered around him, looking down at him, while Joe produced the pack of ten marihuana cigarets – New Golds, made by P. Lorillard from Choicest Mexican and Asian Leaf.

'No no, just forget it,' Scott said, waving a hand. 'I don't—'

'No no yourself,' Peggy said, pulling his arm and nodding to Nancy, who laid hold of his other wrist with both hands. 'Down on the floor with us, Scotty the Kid, and let's push your ignition button.'

So Scott sat on the floor, cross-legged, and they sat with him, the four of them very close, with Peggy pressed against his right side and Nancy his left and Joe's folded knees touching his and Joe's intent face a few inches away. Scott smoked the second cup, while the others shared one.

'Why cup?' he asked.

'Tea,' Peggy said. Peggy knew everything, Scott thought. And she was so warm; he could feel every inch of her skin against him, and he could even feel the fine hairs on her arm, and on Nancy's too, come to think, and he'd never before been so aware of the beat of his own heart. 'Cuppa tea.'

'What do people ignite with where you come from, Scotty?' Joe asked, and Scott noticed that he was speaking very slowly and clearly, enunciating not only each syllable but each letter in each word. Scott squinted, starting to count the hairs in Joe's mustache; fascinating.

'Uh – we drink,' Scott said, sucking in another long drag with the little "ffft" sound they had taught him, and realizing that the reason he seemed to have three heartbeats was that he could feel both Nancy's and Peggy's. They were out of time, a little faster than his own. He started to count them, all three, to see how many beats each of them had per minute.

'God,' Joe said, 'that's poison,' and Scott noticed the way Joe's tongue lapped the backs of his upper teeth when he pronounced the 'n'. That stuff's poison!'

Peggy giggled, rather slowly, Scott mused, enjoying the feel of her left nipple rubbing up and down on his right upper arm, riffling each hair in turn. He felt every one. She put an arm around him and the other arm around Joe, and Joe put an arm around her and one around Nancy – Scott felt his fingers just for a moment – and Nancy slid an arm around Scott and another one around Joe. They leaned in. Scott felt the girl's cheeks against his, noticed that Peggy's nipple against his arm was harder and longer, and that Nancy's breast against his other arm was hard and soft at once. He was glad she'd sat on his left, so that it was her right breast, the mostly bare one, against his arm.

'Joe doesn't drink at all,' Peggy said, after giggling for about ten minutes, and it took another five minutes to say it, too.

'Is it having an effect now, Scott?' Nancy asked, and she too was speaking very distinctly; he could practically count a beat between each word. The words seemed blue; Peggy talked yellow and Joe's were sort of brown and green or maybe reddish.

'I don't think so,' Scott told her, noticing how slowly he was talking, and how he could hear the words inside his head, as if he had his hands over his ears. He concentrated on talking faster: 'What am I supposed to feel?' But he didn't seem to be speaking much more rapidly. His heart had slowed down, too. Noticing a tendril of smoke floating in a glow of blue light, he squinted, seeing that the tendril was composed of many smaller filaments. He started to count them.

All of the clothing, his and theirs, was terribly coarse, and he thought as they all undressed that it was really a terrible shame people couldn't make softer clothing, but skin was softer, and Nancy's breasts very soft indeed, and they tasted lovely, sort of pale blue, and he felt it all over his body and all through his body when he went into her, and he was surprised, later, to realize how long it had taken, because he had had a fearful thought at the back of his mind that he would be embarrassingly fast, since he was a virgin because handjobs didn't count. But even so he saw that Joe took a lot longer, and Nancy seemed to wish he had, and she played with him and pulled his hands onto her, and the rug was very coarse but that wasn't so bad, it merely made skin seem all the softer, and when Joe kissed Nancy and Scott turned his head to find Peggys' face approaching him through a blue haze, ever so slowly, he let his eyelids sag and kissed her and her hands replaced Nancy's on him and after a while his moved to Peggy and that time he took a lot longer, and he was very pleased with himself, although hc wished her fingernails weren't tearing all those ribbons out of his back. She made him jump a little when she screamed and clutched him even more tightly, but he had read and heard some things and seen Andy with Suzanne in the woods, and he heard Joe's laughing snort, and he knew it was all right, it was just that he was a big strong self-controlled male and she was There, that was all, but shortly thereafter he was no longer self-controlled and it seemed to take five or ten minutes to pump it all out, after which he went almost immediately to sleep, both on and in Peggy.

Chapter Eighteen

Scott awoke feeling great, wonderful, marvelous, although a little light of head. He was lying on the rug on his back.

He could feel it all along his body, including low on his back and on his buttocks and the backs of his thighs, which meant he was naked. He closed his eyes and thought about it. Then he rememberd. He tried to concentrate on it, all of it, tried to remember, but there were distractions.

It was the com beside the door, buzzing. Peggy walked long-leggedly to it as he looked. Naked, her bottom didn't look so good; Peggy, he mused, was the sort of girl who should wear clothes as much as possible. She opened the com.

'For god's sake open the doors we're being ATTACKED!'

It was a man's voice, yelling, almost screaming, and mingled in with it was a woman's voice, also screaming but not pronouncing words.

Scott was off the floor and jerking on his trousers before Peggy started depressing keys. To his left Nancy jerked to an erect sitting position.

'PEGGY! Don't open it – *they'll* get in too!'

Peggy glanced around, frowning, confused, and her eyes widened as she saw that Scott already had on his trousers and was sliding into his shirt at the same time as he thrust a sock-clad foot into his short black boot. And he was glancing around, noting where his belt and holster hung.

'You open that damned door, Peggy,' he snapped, talking like Jeff Andrews and planning already what had to be done. 'They'll tell you when they're in, and they can shut it themselves from inside the car, can't they?'

'Yes—'

Scott bent to buckle his boots. 'Then open that damned door!'

Peggy stared at him a moment before nodding and turning back to the controls. Her hands moved swiftly. Joe was sitting up, gazing blankly around. Nancy was sobbing.

'Joe: get up and dress fast. Nancy: shut up and get something on. Peggy: yell or sound the alarm in the Common Room or whatever it is you do.' Scott strode toward her, buckling on the heavy belt. 'And open this door.'

He neither saw nor heard anyone or anything as he ran

down the carpeted hallway. He remembered which way the elevator was, and he knew how to punch a button marked B. The doors sighed shut. He gasped as he shot downward and his stomach shot up into his chest. He tried to absorb it by bending his legs, then remembered that was what you did when you hit bottom, but by the time he had straightened and was ready to flex again to absorb the shock, he was gasping as the elevator came to a stop. B, the light above the doors said. He pawed at them, grunting and straining, but they opened only when they were ready.

He stepped out into the garage basement. And noise.

Male voices, yelling at each other and cursing and laughing. A female voice, shrieking. Feet slapping the concrete floor.

Two males in dark blue jackets were coming for him; behind them a minik squatted in the middle of the floor, with both doors hanging open and the windshield and the glass on one side smashed. One of the two approaching him with fixed eyes hefted a longish, heavy-looking section of pipe. The other, a huge man with wild dark hair, carried a big-bladed knife.

'Get back,' Scott said. 'Get the hell back!'

The big one laughed, carrying the knife low, ready to stab in and up rather than down; he knew how to use it. The other one frowned, but rolled his eyes at his partner and kept coming. His knuckles were white around the pipe.

Behind Scott, the elevator doors closed and he heard its internal clicks and belches as it prepared to go back up. The minik was twenty feet away; the two baboons ten . . . nine. . . .

Scott leveled his gun. 'Dammit, STOP!'

'My god, Horse, he's got a gun!'

Horse sidestepped twice, widening the distance between himself and his comrade, and went into a crouch. His eyes were on Scott's face.

'Careful, boy,' he said. 'You shoot him I'm on you. Shoot me and get your arm broke with that pipe. Be ready to smash his sinkin' arm, Chucko!'

Chucko went into a crouch, his eyes on the gun.

'Not one more step,' Scott said, not daring to glance in the direction of the feminine screams. They stopped.

'WHAT THE HELL'S GOING ON OVER THERE?' a voice bellowed, echoing and re-echoing in the basement-garage that ran the length and breadth of the building. 'HORSE?'

'Some joker with a gun,' Horse called, and moved, fast, straight in, his right arm sweeping out toward Scott. Light flashed from the knife's tip.

BLOOMMMMMM!

The shot was loud in Scott's ears, loud and echoic in the basement, but he didn't stop to check its results. He merely sidestepped. Twitched his hand to the right. Squeezed again. BLOOM!

Horse's knife scraped the closed elevator door; Horse's knuckles rapped it; Horse's head thudded against it. Horse slid down, grunting and gasping and curling fetally. The knife lay on the floor. He had dropped it to clutch his belly, trying to hold back the dark red glisten that crept between his fingers.

The second shot rocked the second attacker, and for a moment he stood there, crouching, staring at Scott. Then his eyes glassed and he dropped to his knees. The pipe rang off the floor. It made a *wolla-wolla-wolla* sound as it rolled away. He fell forward.

Scott was already moving toward the other voice, toward where he'd heard the woman screaming. A man lay on his stomach six or seven feet away from the car, with a little red puddle creeping from beneath him. Another, a total bloody-battered mess, lay just beside the car, where they'd dragged him out and beaten and stabbed him to death. Scott wondered, fleetingly, which was that girl Helen Caudill's father.

Someone fired at him, a spatting sound that was probably a .32, and he ducked sidewise and down, at the minik's hood. He crouched there for just a moment, then pushed back from it and dropped flat to peer beneath.

There were several. One was in the corner, by the door controls, a man in red shirt and pants beneath his dark blue jacket. Another was on his belly just a few feet away, writhing – no he wasn't. He was on someone else's belly, whoever belonged to the feet upturned on either side of his. And he was hunching, not writhing. Wishing he would raise himself enough to receive a bullet between the shoulders, Scott flicked his eyes. That one stood over a crumpled, twisted body that was very white; Scott assumed the dark little patches and blobs here and there on the floor were clothing. Hers, and the man's; he wore no pants. He held a knife. It was dark, smeary. He'll keep, Scott thought instantly, and kept looking.

The man with the gun stood in a tiny wreath of smoke, staring at the minik. Smoke from the gun, Scott thought, and gauged the distance to be twenty or twenty-five feet. All of them were down near the outer doors. He used both hands, resting the heels on the floor with the gun butt between them, and fired, one-two.

The man spun around twice and fell, and Scott wished he'd fired only once.

'D-a-d-d-y . . .' Horse was groaning in a tiny voice. 'Da-ad-dee. . . .'

'Good god, Turko, get the hell off her,' the one by the door said, 'he's shot Vic too!'

Good man, Scott thought, and wiggled a little to get a good line on Turko as he rose. The woman's feet were still. Scott waited until Turko turned his way, presenting a broader and therefore better target, and then he shot him in the stomach, as low as he dared. He hoped sincerely he'd blown his damned genitals off, but had been afraid to aim that low. Three bullets left; he couldn't afford misses.

Something glowed in the darker corner opposite the one by the controls. There was a hiss; Scott felt heat. He heard the car respond with a louder hiss.

My god, he thought, one of them's got a defenser, and he turned his gun and emptied it at the glow, BLOOM BLOOM BLOOM-oom-oom-oom, loud in his ears, loud under the minik, echoing from one wall after the other.

The glow went out and something rattled on the floor.

'How many times he shot?' The voice came from the parked cars; there was another one Scott hadn't seen.

The one beside the controls ran to disappear among the parked miniks and occasional country-car.

'Don't know . . . god! Horse, and Chucko . . . Turko and Vic . . . my god, he's a one-man army!'

Panting, quivering with prickly heat and shivering all over, Scott rolled onto his side, shoving his hand down into his pocket for the bullets there. He withdrew the box, laid his gun down to open it, and started concentrating on taking the cartridges out, on at a time. Which seemed stupid; he needed one in the chamber first. He picked the gun up and emptied the chambers onto the floor, wincing at each clink. Thrusting in one cartridge, he positioned the cylinder. After that he sighed and started pushing in more cartridges, trying to keep an eye on everything at once from under the car.

'We need Mose's laser, dammit! MOSE?'

'Christ, he got Mose too, Damn you, Shanks, you shouldn't have killed Berto. We need a sinkin' ARMY!'

Berto? Scott frowned. Berto? Bert-Ross the brother Peggy and Nancy had mentioned. Helen's brother? Good god, had the girl's parents and brother all been killed on the same night – with her upstairs at an apt party?

Ding, the elevator said, and Scott glanced at it. The doors opened. A girl rushed out, straight into the open hands that Horse closed on her ankle. The girl squeaked and sprawled. Horse hung on, struggling to his knees and pulling her in as he moved.

Scott recognized the girl: Helen Caudill.

Scott aimed; the girl was in the way. He scooted to his feet and dived, gun and all, straight into her. She squeaked again as he rammed into her, one arm on either side of her body. Both of them went down on top of Horse, who screamed like a woman. Scott's gun clattered on the concrete; Scott grunted as his knuckles struck it. Then he twisted his wrist and pushed with it, lying on the girl, until the gun's muzzle touched something. It yielded. Scott pulled the trigger, twice.

Then he rolled off the sobbing girl and got quickly up, glancing at the basement's front end again, his eyes sweeping the snouts of the parked cars along the side wall. No one. He looked down.

Horse's eyes were wide open, but they weren't staring at him. They weren't staring at anything. Panting, Scott leaned down to wrap his fingers around the girl's arm. The elevator door started to close behind him, and he released her arm to lurch forward against the button. The doors shuddered, jerked, stopped, retreated. Scott glanced around, considered wedging Horse's body in the doorway. Then he stepped into the elevator to search for the door-locking mechanism. There wasn't one. For the safety of the dwellers in this goddam cave-castle, he thought, and slapped the Open button as the doors started to close again. Then he stepped out. Clenching his teeth, he seized Horse's shoulders.

He wedged the corpse in the doorway.

Scott's eyes rose as he did, and he made a face. The girl was on her hands and knees, vomiting. There was blood all over the back of her blouse and a little on her shorts. From Horse's belly, of course. Scott stepped out to her.

He stop-crouched in mid-step, swinging the pistol at the movement his peripheral vision announced. There were three of them, side by side, running on silent gym-shoes toward the girl, toward him. Their eyes snapped wide. They stopped, one stumbling over the feet of the one just in front of him and falling. The first one dropped the knife he held in his left hand, dropped the piece of pipe he held in his right. His hands shot up beside his head. The one beside him glanced at him, then dropped his weapons, another knife and length of pipe. The fallen man just stared at Scott's gun. He started to weep.

'Don't shoot, fella,' the first one said. Scott recognized the voice of the leader, the one who'd been over by the controls. 'You've got us.'

'Dammit,' Scott heard himself snarl, a hideous sound from the throat, 'dammit damn you you filthy murdering bastards JUMP me! For god's sake JUMP me so I can SHOOT!'

Wide-eyed, open-mouthed, the leader and the man beside him held their hands straight up, hands stretched, fingers straight to the vertical. Their arms quivered.

'We give up! You've got us! Please don't shoot!'

Scott chewed into his lip; oh damn them damn them damn them, damn himself; Dad would shoot them, surely, what in the name of anything, anything at all, were these three monsters worth, and what kind of asshole code have we spawned that I stand here and can't KILL them?

But he didn't kill them. 'Sit down,' he said. 'I SAID SIT DOWN'

'DADDY!'

The two were starting to sit, frowning, trying to do it without taking their hands down, pale and trembly with fear. Scott glanced down; the girl was crawling, *crawling* over to the man beside the minik.

'Helen,' Scott said. She kept crawling. 'Helen!' She reached the battered little bag of bloody flesh that had been a man, a man who had yelled *For god's sake open the doors we're being attacked,* and who had sat there helplessly while they smashed his car, and had seen the doors open and jammed his hand forward and raced inside and slammed the doors – too late, too late to save himself or the Frasers or his wife.

'Daddy!'

'Helen,' Scott said, glancing at the trio of blue-jacketed baboons; they were all sitting, hands up, staring at him. All they needed were their hands over eyes, ears, and mouths. 'Helen don't—'

'Oh no they killed my daddy Daddy Daddy. . . .'

Scott concentrated on taking one deep breath after the other. He saw a blur, squeezed his eyes tight shut and felt the ears, warm on his cheek's. *Damn!* How could a man be a man when he couldn't help crying, for god's sake?

Helen had clutched the body of her father, had fallen forward onto it. Now she rose to her knees, half-turning; she was a mass of blood, blouse and shorts and arms and bare thighs. Knowing that none of it was hers made it no less hideous. She stared at Scott. Glanced at the seated trio.

'They killed my daddy.' It was a little girl's voice.

'Helen, please come back over here,' Scott said. 'You've got to call the police or open the doors or whatever it is you people do. I've got these three. Just come over here, honey,' he said, as if he were talking to a child – and hoping, hoping, *willing* that she would come, that she would not glance around and then rush or even worse *crawl* to where the two women lay, unmoving.

'Berto's . . . sister,' one of the three rippers grunted. He was the one who had fallen; his face was dead white.

She looked at him. 'Berto? Bert? My brother Bert?' She stood up. 'You know my brother Bert?' She started toward them.

Scott moved to intercept her. 'Helen!'

'You know my brother Bert-Ross?' Still the child's voice.

The man – now looking very much a boy, not the swaggering baboon he had been – started shivering violently. His eyes rolled. His teeth chattered. His eyes swung to the man beside him, the leader.

'He – Shanks—'

'Shut up, Keys!'

'He – he—'

Shanks dropped one arm just enough to ram an elbow into Keys' cheek. Keys toppled sideways as Scott raised the gun. Staring at it, Shanks stretched both arms ceilingward.

'He – killed . . . Berto,' Keys said, as if he were in hypnosis, as if he were clutched by a compulsion commanding him to speak, to accuse someone of something he had not done. 'Berto – saw they were his own folks, and he – he – he wouldn't . . . Shanks killed him.'

The shivering, blood-smeared girl stood staring at them. She turned just as he reached for her arm. He frowned as he saw her face. It looked perfectly calm.

'Give me the gun,' she said, 'and go down there and

push the red lever down to open the doors. See the light flashing? Someone called the police, and if we don't open the door they'll burn it open.'

'You – Helen you go, I can't give—' Scott was frowning, trying to look through her eyes into her mind. Her voice sounded as calm as she looked, exactly as it had when she'd come to Nancy and Peggy's door; perhaps a little quieter and more calm; then she'd been on her way to a party.

She stretched out her hand. 'I'll watch them,' she said. 'Hurry – don't let them burn the doors open!'

Her hand touched his, touched the gun. Scott's teeth sank into his lip. His hand loosened....

'Hurry,' the girl said and Scott let her have the gun and she nodded and glanced at the three seated baboons and Scott set off for the other end of the basement, sprinting, and by the time he reached the wall and his hand closed around the red lever his gun had roared four times and was clicking, clicking, clicking on empty chambers.

Chapter Nineteen

'Scott? What're you reading?'

Scott looked up, then rose sinuously, folding the book over his thumb in an automatic movement. 'Hi! Your book.' He held it up.

She came over to look at it. 'Oh – *Quo in Arco Vadimus?* You know what that means?'

'Sure,' he said. 'I've read it before.'

'Oh.' She looked around, then turned toward him again, biting her lip. 'Is this the way you've been acting all along?'

'Hmm?'

'What day is this?'

'Uh – Sunday—'

'The date—'

'Oh. The fourteenth.'

'And when did it . . . happen?'

Scott pursed his lips, studying her face, then said, 'The eighth.'

She nodded, narrowing her eyes. 'Six days . . . god. And you've been here all along, I know that.' She fixed his eyes with those bright blue ones of hers. 'Scotty . . . what . . . what have I been like?'

He stepped back and sat down in a rush. 'You're back.'

She nodded, glancing around the room. 'I'm back. I have some sort of memories . . . I know you've been here and I've been as if I were in, uh, in some sort of mist, or something. Here, but not here. What have I been like?'

'Like a little girl, Helen.'

'Tell me about it.' She pulled a fat, warmly brown cushion over to his chair and sat on it. She stared into his eyes. 'Tell me about it, Scott.'

'Suppose you tell me what you remember, Helen. If – damn, I don't know. Do you think you should?'

'I remember,' she said.

Scott wondered. Did she remember all of it? Yes, her parents were dead, and her brother. But did she remember tricking him out of his gun – he supposed it was a trick – and shooting the three kneeling rippers with their hands up? Did she remember her mother, and all the seeping blood and semen?

As if she were reading his mind, she said, 'I remember shooting those three . . . and I remember mother. . . .' She shuddered, carefully not-looking at him. She frowned 'But then I can't recall anything else. . . .'

He had opened the doors. The Fep truck had gunned in, along with a smaller vehicle containing four local police. Quickly establishing that the danger to other residents of the building was ended, that this was a small affair and not a demo, the Fep had departed. There were merely a dozen bodies or so, entirely within the jurisdiction and coping powers of the local police. Elsewhere there was real trouble.

'Somebody did a fine job on all these baboons,' the

sergeant had said. He turned to Scott, gazing questioningly at him.

Scott nodded. 'I did.'

They shook their heads, reexamined the bodies, and questioned him. They tried to ignore the little girl in the young woman's body who wandered about the basement, all over blood. They had established that the blood was not hers, any of it. One of them dragged Horse's body out of the elevator, which immediately closed and went up. A minute or so later it returned. There were two men, each with a gun.

'What's the trouble?' one of them asked.

'Who are you gentlemen?' the sergeant asked.

They were residents. They had been at the apt party.

'Get the hell back up to your little cage castles,' Scott yelled. 'Where the hell were you bastards when your neighbors needed you?' He swung his arm, finger stabbing like a dagger. 'They killed Caudill and that other man, Fraser. Beat them to death. They killed their wives, more slowly, with knives, and they raped them. Look at her.' He pointed at Helen. She glanced up blankly, smiling a little. 'My god, it's been twenty or thirty minutes! Where *were* you bastards?'

'Who's this punk?' one of the men asked.

'One of the rippers, obviously,' the other one said, raising his gun. It was a recently made, high-voltage defenser.

'Hold it now,' the sergeant said. He jerked a thumb at Scott. 'This young man saved the girl, probably saved you and your wives. There seem to have been seven rippers, not counting the one they killed themselves.' His voice was a little incredulous as he said, 'This young man seems to have got them all – and he isn't even wounded.'

The two men from upstairs stared at Scott as if he were an animal.

'We called the police,' one of them said. 'We did something.'

'Only an idiot would have rushed down here, right into the middle of who-knows-what.'

The sergeant stood close beside Scott. 'You're right,' he said. 'Only an idiot would have rushed down here.' He glanced at Scott. 'Thank god for idiots in this damned world.' He was about twenty-two, Scott thought.

'Well – look here, are you saying—'

'GET THE HELL BACK UPSTAIRS!' Scott bellowed. 'We don't need you. The Caudills and the Frasers don't need you! Helen doesn't need you, and I don't, and these policemen sure don't!'

'Officer, we *live* here. You aren't going to stand there and let this young animal—'

'You two gentlemen had better go on back upstairs,' the sergeant said. 'We'll take care of all this.' He waved a hand; all this was a ghastly, an unbelievable number of dead bodies.

The two men reentered the elevator. They took their guns and their bravery and their muttering and their spiteful looks at Scott back upstairs with them.

'Where are you from?' the sergeant asked.

'Morehead,' Scott said. 'Out of town. Out in the country, I mean.'

The sergeant nodded. 'Ah, that's it. You just didn't know. In a city, cowardice is the better part of valor. Keep your nose clean, that's the way. Stay out of it; don't get involved. You're right. Obviously a gang of people could have rushed down here from the apt party and taken this gang apart, or scared them off, weapons or not. They didn't. Those two men are probably the bravest in the whole damned building.'

'They waited thirty minutes!'

'Well, a little less,' the sergeant said. He shrugged. 'Anyhow, you stay around here you'll get killed, playing Lone Ranger and trying to help other people out. It's our business. A few years ago you'd have been in all sorts of trouble. Hearings, trials, bond or jail, endless questions and pretrial by newspaper.'

Scott stared at him. 'For rushing down to help some people?' He shook his head. 'I wasn't even in time.'

'Yes,' the sergeant said, 'for rushing down to help some

people. I remember a case we studied where a whole batch of people, I mean like twenty or thirty, watched a girl get raped and listened to her screams while the rapist stabbed her to death. She actually got away from him once and ran to a door. No one opened it. He stabbed her to death there, in plain sight. I don't remember her name; something Italian. There was another case about a girl who defended herself with a switchblade knife. She was booked; it's an illegal weapon.'

'She should have let herself be raped and killed?'

The sergeant shrugged. 'It's the American way. You ever see a TV hero draw the fire first? Of course not. We've been waiting for forty or fifty years for Russia or China to attack us. They've spent that time getting ready, catching up to us. . . .' He shrugged again, looking around. His cohorts had called a meat-wagon and were lining up the bodies so they'd be ready to load swiftly and efficiently when the truck arrived. The girl was talking to her mother's corpse, in a little-girl voice.

'There was some guy out west someplace, a farmer who'd been broken in on several times. So he rigged up a shotgun, I think it was, to fire when somebody came through the window. Somebody did, a ripper. The shotgun went off. It didn't kill him. The ripper sued.'

Scott snorted. That was too ridiculously incredible to think about.

'The ripper won,' the sergeant said, watching Helen with a little line between his brows. Maybe he was thirty, Scott thought.

'What?'

The sergeant nodded. 'The farmer and his wife had to auction their place to get the money to pay off the ripper.'

Scott stood there, looking around, noting the blood and weapons on the floor, thinking about the attack on the food truck he'd ridden, about the two toughs on the sidewalk, and how Nancy had pulled him aside so they could swagger on by without confrontation, without any challenge to their assumption of ownership of the sidewalk. He thought about Janie, and about the attempted rip-off on the

Andrews place a couple of months ago, and about the two men on the elevator. He watched Helen, and he felt sick.

'That's why things're the way they are,' he said.

The sergeant dropped a hand on his shoulder, shaking his head. 'Naw . . . it's population. There're too many of us.'

Scott looked intensely at him. 'Yes, sure . . . but if we learned or were taught or forced or frightened out of protecting ourselves, by the things you mentioned . . . then that's the big reason.'

'Maybe,' the sergeant said, walking over to pick up the empty .45 revolver. He hefted it, examined it, sniffed, made a face. He spun the cylinder, looked questioningly at Scott.

'Every one of them, 'Scott said.

The sergeant gave his head that amazed shake again. 'You have more bullets?'

Scott nodded.

The sergeant handed him the pistol. 'Better load up. You're one hell of a shot. I kind of like the idea that you're around. Wish you'd move into my apt. Got a wife and daughter over there.' He smiled. 'Back to what you said – maybe. But remember, things aren't that way anymore. Criminals used to have rights. Now they don't. There are too many of them, too many of everybody except us' – he patted his badge, dropped his hand – 'to be able to worry about John Doe's rights, much less nightscum like these. As a country, we overkilled. We hired so many minority-group members that in the seventies we had all that WASP trouble; they couldn't get jobs. We protected criminals, both accused and convicted, so much that we bred more of them. Along with everything else,' he added, forestalling Scott's mention of overpop.

'So here we are, Scott Andrews. You and that girl, and eleven bodies.'

'Twelve. There's one over there among those empty barrels.'

The sergeant stared at him. 'With a .45 hole in him?'

Scott nodded, looking away. 'Several, I think.'

'Clayton,' the sergeant said, and one of the policemen

looked up. He was gathering weapons. 'There's another one.' The sergeant pointed. With a look at Scott, Clayton went over to the corner where the man with the laser had been.

'Will I have to go with you?' Scott asked.

'Where are you staying?'

'Uh – here?'

'Will you keep an eye on that girl? She wasn't like this – before, was she?'

Scott shook his head. 'No, she wasn't. Yes I will.'

'OK. No, we don't need you. We've got your name if we need to add to our report. These—' He swung a hand, let it drop. 'These we burn. Someday we'll get sense enough to stick em in the ground without boxes, let them fertilize the soil. No, we won't need you, Scott Andrews. Come down and apply for a job. Name's Hargis.' He stuck out his hand.

'Hi, Hargis.'

'Hi, Andrews. You're tough. Either join us or get the hell back where you came from. Grow me some food.' He slapped his flat gut. 'I could use some more meat. Your dad raise cows?'

Scott shook his head, watching the big tan truck nose slowly into the basement garage. Its double side doors swung open. Four tan-uniformed men dropped out, looked around, shook their heads, and began very efficiently to load the bodies into the truck. The driver and the man in white came over to Scott and Sergeant Hargis.

Hargis explained quickly; both the driver and the doctor gave Scott looks.

'You're a one-man army, son,' the doctor said.

'That's what their leader said,' Scott told him quietly.

'Which one was that?' The doctor glanced toward the truck; the sixth ripper was being slid in.

'The one with the hole where his left eye was,' Scott said, thinking that Helen had used the gun pretty damned well. 'Name was Shanks, I think.'

The sergeant nodded. 'Shanks, yes. He's credited with a

lot, him and his Hawks. Should've been stillborn. Thanks from the city.'

The doctor went over to Helen, talked nicely to her, as if he were the first-grade teacher and Helen was there on the first day. He looked into her eyes, checked her pulse, assured himself that none of the blood was hers. He came back to them.

'She should go with us,' he said. 'She needs a sedative and hospitalization.'

'No,' Scott snapped, then looked a little embarrassed. 'I mean – give her the sedative, and leave medicine or tell me what to do. She stays.'

The doctor glanced at Sergeant Hargis, back at Scott. 'Who's her next of kin?'

'One of the men is her father, the bigger one. Was, I mean. And one of the women is her mother, the one with – one of them. The one in the red shirt is her brother.'

'Jesus – was he with the rippers?'

'No,' Scott said, and Hargis stared at him. Scott ignored him.

'And you?'

'I'm her cousin,' Scott said, ignoring Hargins' stare. 'I'll take care of her. Tell me what to do, and give me a number to call, and a name, will you, Doctor? I think she's better off here.'

The doctor looked at Sergeant Hargis. Hargis gazed at Scott a moment longer, then looked at the doctor.

'Yes,' he said. 'Her cousin. Why don't you give him the clinic number, and Doc Messer's name.'

'Right – and a sedative. Let's get her back upstairs to her apt, and let me give her some sedation and write out some things for this young man. For her cousin.'

So they took Helen back upstairs, and fortunately she remembered her apt number, because it would have been very difficult and embarrassing for Scott; he had no idea where she lived. On seventeen, that was all he knew. The same floor with Nancy and Peggy. Nancy and Peggy! What a night this had been! He'd become a man in more ways than one!

'I've been giving you the medicine he ordered,' Scott told Helen Caudill, six days later. 'I've had to call the clinic twice. Oh you haven't been difficult or anything. But I wanted to be careful. I knew you'd come out of it. I didn't want to do anything to stop that.'

She sat on the little upholstered stool beside his chair, looking up at him. Clear, clear blue eyes. The eyes of a little girl – except now, thank god, there was light in them, not the blankness, not the childlike gaze. She was back.

'You seem to have done about everything.'

'I've just stayed here.' Scott shrugged. 'The money for the food I've ordered, and the medicine, was your money. Your . . . inheritance, you know. I had to have some help on that. It worked out; the grocery just said they'd wait until it was cleared up.' He smiled, just a little. 'I imagine they have a lien against your account, though.' He'd almost said 'your parents' account. He was afraid to mention them.

'Dad . . . and mother?'

'Recycled.' He gazed at her. She flinched only a little.

'And . . . Bert-Ross?'

'With them,' Scott told her.

She stared at his face a moment longer, the big blue eyes wide, then she threw her arms around his legs, pressing herself to them. He was very much aware of her bosom. He'd been aware of it and several other things, for six days. It hadn't exactly been easy. Particularly not on the night when she'd had the dreams, and he'd had to comfort her, and she'd begged him to sleep with her. He had. She had gone to sleep at once, happy child; he had not, because she was a child only in her mind. Or two days ago, when she'd come out of the bathroom naked, wanting to know where he'd put her clothes. He hadn't put them anywhere; it was a child's question. But it was not a child's bouncy, hip-swaying body, jiggling temptingly as she walked, as if the naked breasts were on rubber strings attached to the ceiling.

'Thank you,' she said. 'Thank you!' She was weeping, but it did not sound like a child's sobbing.

He touched her head, stroked her hair. 'I didn't tell them about him,' he said. 'They called him Berto. The rippers, I mean.'

She nodded against his leg. 'I remember.'

'I didn't tell them about him. I lied. I told them he and I ran down to try to help your—' He stopped, bit his lip, then said it '– your parents, and the rippers killed him. I think Sergeant Hargis knows better. He's a hell of a nice guy.'

She nodded against his legs, holding on to them. 'Won't – won't they check further? I mean – a sergeant isn't very high up.'

'Anyone,' Scott said, staring at the wall and thinking about all he'd read and all the skull-sessions he'd had with himself this week, 'anyone, anywhere who will take charge is authority enough. The police are too busy to check further. Just – I'm sorry, Helen – just five more people murdered by baboons, and a batch of baboons dead and got rid of, to be replaced by twice as many the next day, probably.' His hand tightened on her head. He could feel the skull through the softness of her hair. It felt funny; round and hard and small, defenseless, as if without the hair she would be far more vulnerable. He supposed she would.

'One more girl,' he said, 'with a case of hysterics. I could tell that the people at the clinic were as busy as the police. And the drugstore didn't want to send the medicine. So I dropped some names, Sergeant Hargis and Dr. Clark and Dr. Messer. No go. Then I had sense enough to hang up. I called back and got Nancy to bring the stuff home with her. Dr. Clark had left an ampule – that was the hardest part, giving you another shot – and some capsules and pills, just a few.'

She sat back from his legs, her eyes swimming in tears. She squeezed them tight shut and jerked her head to hurl them from her, then wiped the last of the moisture away with her fingertips.

'Nancy? She brought the . . . medicine?'

He nodded.

'And – and you and I have been here a week . . . nearly . . . just the two of us . . . in. . . .' She glanced around, 'Here.'

He nodded. Then he smiled his slow, quiet smile. It was modeled after Alex's; everything Alex did was slow and quiet, while Jeff Andrews' smile was huge as his laughter.

'And you, and I, and everything else is just like it was,' he said.

She flushed. 'It's been awfully hard for you,' she said, after a long reflective silence.

'Oh, not too tough – yeah. It's been hard. You're a doll.'

She looked up at him, smiled. 'Where – where have you slept?'

He leaned out to pat the couch. 'And you in there, in your own bed.'

She was frowning. 'I remember . . . my gosh do I remember . . . ?' She flushed again.

He nodded 'You remember. And nothing happened, either. It was hard, I'll tell you that. I hope I don't ever have to sleep with a woman again, playing brother and sister.'

'A . . . woman.' She thought about that. 'I'm sorry, Scott.'

'Don't tell me you're sorry, Helen,' he said, leaning over her. 'You don't bother to feel sorry for me, and—'

She stopped him, putting a hand on his leg. 'All right,' she said. 'If you'll stop feeling sorry for me.'

'God, how can I?'

They sat looking into each other's eyes. 'I'll make it,' she said.

He nodded. 'I believe you.'

They sat in silence for a long time. He was eminently aware of her hand on his leg; when she became conscious of it, she removed it.

'Scotty. . . .'

He answered her by being silent, waiting.

'Scotty . . . how long . . . how long can you stay?' She wasn't looking at him.

He snorted. 'I got to town the day before I met you. The

first night I spent with the guy who drove the food truck I hitched a ride in. The second night, and since then . . . here. I don't have an apartment, and I had a job I haven't showed up for. I called. It was charity anyhow, I think. We don't accept charity, where I come from. Don't say anything; we've traded evenly, you and I. I've been parent and guardian and doctor, but it's your apt and your money for the food and so on.' And he added, as she seemed to be about to ignore his mandate, '*Don't* say anything.'

'All right, but that doesn't answer my question.'

'What – oh. How long can I stay. Well, I was telling you I'm not staying away from anywhere or anything. Or anyone. What—'

'Where are you from?'

He told her, and she frowned, and then looked at the book he'd been reading, and back at him.

'That's where he lives. Jefferson Andrews.'

He nodded. 'My father.'

'My gosh. I've read probably a half-dozen of his novels, and I know there are some of the old ones Dad won't let me read—' She came to a full stop, corrected herself carefully, pedantically. 'My father wouldn't let me read some of the older ones.' She nodded at *Quo In Arco Vadimus*. 'I think that's just brilliant.'

He nodded. 'So do I. I've read it a little more objectively, here, away from him. We've never been exactly buddies. Yeah, he's a bright guy. I've read a lot of your books, probably twenty since I've been here, including his.' He made an apologetic gesture at her expression; impressed/disbelief. 'We don't care much for TV.'

'My gosh. Jefferson Andrews.'

'A man with a beard and three kids – four but my little sister was killed by rippers – and a pretty wife and a little acreage with all sorts of defenses. He shouldn't even be on a "farm", if you can call the place a farm. He should be locked up in a city someplace, in an apartment, never going out. He's a writer, not a man to weed tomatoes and hoe potato-hills and go out every morning to check his . . . defenses. He's working on a book now about the psychology of generals, because he says he feels like one, and he hates it. He just isn't sick enough to want to be commander of a bunch of killers.'

'You like him,' she said, looking at him with her head a little on one side.

'He's my father.'

She shook her blond head. 'No no, that doesn't have anything to do with it. You *like* him.'

He thought about it. 'Well, I think a lot of him. I respect him and his mind and his independence. I'm not sure, though, just how much I *like* him. As a friend, I mean.'

'Well, he's older and he's your father. That gets in the way of your being friends. I sort of liked Dad . . . mother was . . . silly. . . .' She looked away and he sat in silence, studiedly not-looking at her, in case she needed to wipe her eyes or something.

'What are you going to do?' she asked, after a long while.

'I've been thinking about that,' he said. 'I think I'll write. Write on! That's Dad's motto. I believe I can. I'm going to try.'

'Really?' She was gazing into his eyes again, a woman.

He nodded. 'I'm going to try.'

'Locked up in an apartment in a city?'

'No. I won't live in a city either. He indoctrinated us, of course, and now I've been here.' He shook his head. 'No. No cities for me, ever.'

'All that takes us back to my question – how long can you stay. Good grass! Jefferson Andrews' son!'

'Not very long,' Scott told her.

'I . . . guess . . . guess not,' she said quietly, staring at the doorway into the kitchen. 'I shouldn't have thought . . . I mean you could just . . . I've got a scholarship to Harvard starting next month, and—'

'Lord, that's marvelous. I thought you were smart, from the books around the house. I've had a hell of a time staying out of your notebooks.' He added, 'But I have.'

'You'll find quite a bit of Jefferson Andrews in my

notes. You're welcome to look.' She still was not looking at him. 'Are you in school?'

Realizing what each of them knew about the other, and knowing that she knew far less than he, he said, 'Hi. My name's Scott Andrews. I'm seventeen, just. I am a horribly good shot, which seems to be what impresses everybody most.' He watched her shudder, gazing at the kitchen doorway. 'I'm more impressed with my brain, though. Yes, I'm in school; I'm halfway through college.'

'At *seventeen?*' She jerked her wide blue eyes to his face again.

He nodded, feeling himself growing, sure he was rapidly approaching nine feet in height – and knowing that when they stood up he'd still be less than an inch taller than she. And she looked small and feminine. 'I turned seventeen last month.'

'Gosh, you must be a genius!'

'Uh – imagine growing up in a house full of books, with a man like this in charge—' he slapped the book – 'and where the TV is something you turn on every now and then to look at the news, or because Dad does have this thing about movies. He does a lot of longhand writing in front of TV; says he's crazy about old movies but has to have something to *concentrate* on. So—' He spread his hands. 'Naturally all of us turn on with knowledge. We even have – had – an old-fashioned classroom-type school, with the five of us sitting around Dad.' He frowned. 'Then four, and now Andy's got a girl, or I guess he's married now, and so there are only Kristy and Roger. Dad's schoolroom is shrinking,' he said, in a faraway voice and with a look in his eyes that matched the tone.

'Listen . . . I've got to ask you something Scotty.'

It was important, he knew that from her tone and from the slow, stammering way she said it. 'Questions're easy,' he said, 'but the fact that one's asked is no mandate on me to answer it.'

'Hey that's good.'

'Jeff Andrews,' he said quietly.

'Well . . . I met you at Nancy's. I know she and Peggy

are different from me. Peggy acts like it's a crime to be smart. Anyhow, uh – well, what I want to ask—'

'Nancy and I met that day,' he said. 'In the drugstore. I was buying a respirator.'

But that wasn't her question, he saw. Only a part of it. 'And Nancy's been here, bringing medicine and stuff – and I've been running around like a – a child . . . oh gosh, how awful that must've been for you! Has – has she—' she wasn't looking at him – 'spent much, uh, time here?' She waved a hand vaguely.

'Not much time,' he said, slowly. 'But that's not what you're asking. What you're asking is this: yes, she spent the night one night, because I wouldn't leave. I haven't put a foot outside that door, and I guess I wouldn't have if you'd gone on for a month. Anyhow, that's what you're asking, and yes. There was another time, too, but she went back to her own apt . . . after.'

She sat still gazing away from him, nodding slowly, continuously, as if she'd forgotten she was doing it and was on full automatic.

'Also,' he said, 'I'm a hick, and it was my first time.'

'Me too' she said in a tiny voice. 'I mean, I've never . . . uh, I'm . . . different from Nancy and Peggy.'

'Noticed that,' he said, with a smile in his voice so that she could hear it without having to look at him. She very obviously did not want to.

'Have I been . . . teasing you?'

He snorted. It was a characteristic she already recognized as such his snorting. Jeff Andrews probably did it.

'Not on purpose,' he told her.

'But I have.'

'Sure. You seem to remember some things. Like the night you had the dreams and then insisted that I spend the night with you after we'd got you settled down. I think if there were a hell it would include something like that for male citizens. And. . . .'

'I think I remember . . . didn't I – did I lose my clothes once?'

'You did And I hadn't hidden them either. But I had to

help you find them.' He was silent for a moment, then decided to add, '*That's* probably why Peggy doesn't like you.'

'What? What?' They were still sitting side by side, he in the chair and she on the padded stool, but she had not looked at him for several minutes. 'What? What?' she asked, of the opposite wall.

'You,' he said, 'and Peggy. I mean – try something side by side, and Peggy looks like a, uh, boy. You know.' Now he looked away too, although her eyes were not there to be faced or avoided.

'Oh,' she said, the side of her face reddening, 'oh – thank you.'

'I'm, ah, sorry,' he said, and she looked at him.

'Sorry?'

He waved a hand looking woefully uncomfortable. 'About – Nancy.'

'Oh.' She looked down. 'Well . . . don't be. I – I understand.' And then she jerked her head and her eyes up to his face. 'Listen, I'm going to be very honest, and say something fast, and for heaven's sake don't interrupt, so I can get it out. When I asked how long you could stay: I was thinking, we could just stay here forever. Finish school, and do whatever we're going to do. Particularly when you said you're going to write.' She nodded. 'You will. You will be a writer, Scott. And the way we'll never even have to leave the building, this room. And I thought, good, good, that's good, just us in this nest, like our own little castle, and Scotty will write about it and I'll cook and type or whatever he needs and talk; I know I'm no dummy, and we won't have to worry about something's happening on the streets or in the basement—' she shuddered, but she didn't even pause, her voice just shaking and rushing on – 'or anyplace, because we'll just stay here always. I—'

'Good grass, Helen, we don't even know if we *like* each other!'

'I *told* you not to *interrupt* me!' she flashed, flushing and showing him there could be fire in those ingenuous azure eyes. She waved her hands at him as if she wanted to shake him. She talked on, in the same rush, obviously having to concentrate and control herself to look at him. 'Then I asked about Nancy, and I thought I probably knew what the answer would be, I mean that's natural. And I though gosh, I've been in bed with a boy, and what a shame I wasn't even there to enjoy it, and nothing happened! Well, so let me tell you this – you've *got* to stay here awhile longer, because we've got to get to know each other, just what you said, or maybe I couldn't stand it alone and surely you'd feel guilty if you left, but darnit darnit Scotty, you won't need Nancy anymore.'

She stressed the word 'need' only a little and she kept staring at him until suddenly she bit down into her lip and jumped up and rushed across the room to the kitchen and started making kitcheny noises.

MEANWHILE: IX

A City Is a Helluva Place For Bringing Kids Into The World, But—

'The preemie died,' Nurse Pennington said in a quiet voice.

'Oh, no. Poor little thing. How's the mother?'

'She's fine. She didn't want it anyway.' Pennington didn't need to add the words to make a judgment; her tone and expression did it far more eloquently.

'Its little lungs weren't developed enough, I guess, even in the oxygen tank.'

Nurse Pennington nodded, noted the flashing light, and hurried away to Room 1017. That was the last she thought of it until the flap started. She knew Dr. Calvert was going to do an autopsy, but didn't think anything about it. The child was three months premature, a six-month baby, and there just hadn't been enough there, inside, to enable it to live.

But Dr. Calvert was saying there *had* been.

'We're going to have to do a lot more work,' he said. 'I want every child born in this hospital X-rayed, and as soon as there's another preemie I want that child *watched* in the tank. If he looks like he's laboring for breath, get him out, and get him out fast. Don't call for a doctor, don't make a notation, don't think about it. Just pull him out and *then* make a noise. Is that clear?'

The nurses and interns nodded, looking at each other. Pennington put up her hand, slowly, diffidently. 'Doctor....'

'What is it, Miss Pennington?'

'Doctor . . . was there something . . . what was it about that child that was so . . . unusual? What killed her, I mean?'

'I don't know,' he said, staring at her with eyes like

marbles, as if he were looking right through her as if his sight was somehow refracting, bouncing right back in to examine the interior of his own head.

'Wasn't it lack of full lung development, Doctor?' A male voice; Billy. That is, Dr. Roberts, three-month intern.

'The lungs were fine, Doctor,' Dr. Calvert told him.

'Then what—'

'I have just said I don't know,' Dr. Calvert said. 'I have made a telephone call, and Dr. Bettelheim will be down here within a few hours. I was able to show him enough on the phone to interest him in making the trip. Otherwise I'd have air-expressed him a . . . package.'

A little murmur; Bettelheim! Coming here! The hospital would be in all the news. They all would, or might be, if TV people came in to show the great genius here, rather than merely talking about him and showing him getting off the plane, with a still of him and Dr. Calvert. Bettelheim!

'Look,' Dr. Calvert said, 'I had to tell you this, because I wanted you to know George Curtiss Bettelheim is coming here, and I want to be sure you understood what I want done in the case of a preemie. The other thing is to call me at once. At once, wherever I am. And if one comes in while Doctor Bettelheim's here – for god's sake interrupt us. It will be fine.'

'Doctor . . . pardon me, doctor, but – what did you find? I mean, it will be a matter of record . . . what did you put down as cause of death?'

It was the newest resident, the one who wasn't afraid of anything, who had been here two weeks and had already made both Alice and Idamae, the latter in the narco closet. No one else would have dared ask; they'd merely all have had a look at the notes, at the certificate, or waited until they were told or the News told them.

Dr. Calvert stared at him. For a moment or maybe as long as a minute Miss Pennington thought Dr. Calvert was going to smash him, then and there. She'd seen it happen; Dr. Calvert used his voice and his eyes and his vocabularly the same way he used laser and probes.

'Doctor, ahh . . . Morton,' he said, and Miss Pennington winced, tensing, getting ready for the blast. It didn't come.

'. . . the Cory child possessed a finely developed system of internal plumbing, as well as a finely developed set of lungs – or something like lungs, anyhow.'

'They all frowned at him, questioning him silently, begging for elaboration with their eyes.

Dr. Calvert sighed and started playing with the thermometer he always wore clipped in his pocket. 'As to cause of death . . . I'm not certain. It may have been inability to breathe. It wasn't lack of oxygen.'

'Could – could you conjecture, Doctor?'

Lord, that Morton was a pusher! Attractive, too.

'I could, Doctor, and would instantly place myself in a position where not only my sanity but my judgment would be in question, as well. That would pave the way for bright young men such as yourself to think about moving up *before* the old man dies or retires.' He answered their gasps with a small pale smile. 'Besides, it's hard to find anything like a precedent, a frame of reference. The Cory child. . . .' He took a deep breath, shaking his head. 'The Cory child seems to have grooved on what we call air. Outside air, but there's no way to be certain of that without some experimentation. The Cory child's lungs – and several other items – were . . . different. The Cory child seems to have died as a result of . . . oxygen poisoning. But there's no such animal. Or – hasn't been.'

Chapter Twenty

'I love you, Scott Andrews,' Helen said, sliding her hand down along the sheet to find his hand. She squeezed it. His fingers tightened in response. So strong.

He turned his head a little to look at her rather than at the ceiling. 'Nah. Infatuation. Hero-worship.' He smiled.

She stared into his eyes for a long time, her gaze making

little side trips to study his mouth, his nose, his ears, his hair, his throat, his hairless chest.

'No,' she said at last. 'I love you.'

He moved a little to put his hand again onto the prominent adornments of her chest that he liked so much – and that she had discovered she liked having manipulated and loved. She wondered if the inflamed-looking tip was hardening again, getting longer. Probably.

'OK,' he said. 'You love me. I love you too.'

She hugged him, crawling half-atop his body and squeezing, coaxing his chin out of the way so she could nestle her head beneath it and kiss his throat. It pulsed against her lips, and she kissed the pulse.

His hands moved all over her back, all the way down and over the smooth bulges at its base, all the back up to toy with the silky softness of the hair, curly-wispy at the base of her neck.

'Do you think . . . do you think *all* children will be like that, from now on?'

'Like what?'

She rose above him on one elbow. 'You know. Stop pretending. Like that one they talked about on the News.'

He shook his head. '*They* don't even know,' he said. Bettleheim and that other one—'

'—Calvert—'

'—Calvert both sounded like politicians, trying to say nothing while they were pretending to be saying a lot.'

'Yes, but . . . doesn't it make *sense*?'

'If man's going to survive, maybe it does. I don't know. We'll have to wait and see. That's what they said. We'll have to wait and see, do some checking, and it won't be easy, because most parents are averse to having their just-born brats experimented on.'

She shivered. 'Don't put it that way!'

'Checked over, then,' he said. 'Their euphemism.'

'Will we find out, Scotty? Ummm. Don't do that *now*.'

He chuckled, a nice throaty male sound that made his whole body move so that she could feel it all along his length.

'We'll find out,' he said.

She squeezed him tightly.

'Oh – wait a minute. I see what you mean. You get pretty oblique sometimes, lady. We will *not* find out until they're sure. I will *not* have a child in this goddam world unless it has a better-than-even chance of reaching old age. The previous generation didn't have the guts or the maturity – we've *got* to.'

'It will be that way,' she said, with feminine confidence; nest-building mother-confidence. 'All children will be like that.'

'Able to breathe pollution and groove on it.'

She nodded against his chest. 'Yes! And ours will, Scott. He *will*.'

'Whaddaya mean, ours?'

She came up on her elbow again, looking seriously, wistfully, down into his face. 'Our baby. Our child. Another Andrews. Lord, he'll be a brightun!'

He rolled over, raised himself on an elbow, too, and gazed seriously at her.

'Helen, you heard what I said, and you heard the rest of what they said, too. You were right there during the Special on it. Out of one thousand young couples – that's us – tested, less than half will ever have children, unless they do something like artificial insemination or substitute mother. Out of two thousand people, almost eleven hundred were sterile.'

She nodded in silence, looking fearful, thinking about it.

'As to the other, artificial insemination or sub-mother, like she's sterile and he isn't so he fills up a bottle or something with semen and that's injected into someone who'll bear the child and hand it over to him and his barren wife . . . well. It's already started; you heard what Senator Blair said. I'll bet there'll be legislation against it by the end of the year. Mama Nature's gotten tired of messing around with food shortages and wars and things. and she's started in in earnest. We just won't be having many kids.'

'They'll change the other law—'

He shook his head. 'Betcha they don't. We'll have a combination, and it'll be a good one. First, the population control laws already in force. Next, the – whatever you want to call it; the new natural law – will be right in there helping. About half the people in the world—'

'The world? All they talked about was—'

'You think it's limited to the United States? Since when has Mama Nature ever picked on one particular territory? Aside from weather, I mean.'

She nodded, watching his lips move as he talked.

'About half the people in the world,' Scott went on, talking to the pillow, 'can't have kids naturally. And those that can are limited to two. So first the population falls. The way it should. Then we see where we're going.'

'You think you—'

This time he didn't interrupt; she broke off.

He shook his head. 'No, I don't think I'm sterile, or that you are. I don't know. Oh – infertile, I mean. Anyhow, I don't know. We could find out easily enough. I guess we will. But meanwhile we've already agreed. No kids. Not until they're sure about this . . . this new thing, anyhow.'

He said until, of course, not unless. He was man. Man presumes, assumes. The mandate was laid on him before the race was born: Reproduce. Man abides.

'But that was before . . . before we said . . . Scott?'

'Hm?'

'Are we going to get married?'

'I suppose that's the thing to do,' he said, and she squeezed him again, wiggling, and kissed the hollow of his throat until he grunted; she was cutting off his breath. He wrapped a hand around her to clutch, soft/firm, yielding roundness. She squeaked.

'Listen,' he said, a moment later, 'this thing has the damnedest erectile powers since—'

'—you,' she finished, and she giggled and grabbed, and he laughed and made a yipe noise.

'Do you think you could stand a lot of rooms instead of two and a kitchen, and a lot of people around instead of two or three; like about ten, all living together, Helen?

And being able to go out in the daytime – and with no crowd outside, and air that tastes funny because it isn't quite as poisonous as – this?' He waved a hand, she grabbed it and kissed it.

'I think so,' she said softly. 'I'll try. I *will*.'

'Good,' he said. 'Let's call Dad, then, and tell him we're coming home.'

Recycle.

Also from Magnum Books

ANDREW J. OFFUTT

Messenger of Zhuvastou

In hot pursuit of his beautiful 'fiancée', Earthborn playboy Moris Keniston arrives on the mysterious and hostile planet Sovold. Before he can sample its violent lifestyle and bizarre terrain, or combat the amoral whims of its courts (and blue-haired courtesans) he needs to adopt a suitable disguise.

So with shaved head and skin dyed beige, he dons the yellow-crested helmet and green cloak of a Messenger of the mighty empire of Zhuvastou. Armed only with a heavy sword he is ready to set out on his urgent quest . . .

PHILIP K. DICK

The Unteleported Man

Nobody would go to Whale's Mouth the long way when you could travel to this new planetary utopia by instant-teleportation. That is, nobody reasonable would want to spend eighteen long years in a spaceship to get there. Which is what made Rachmael ben Applebaum such a thorn in the side of the giant industrial combine that had made the Telpor what it was. Because Rachmael intended to travel to the colony by his own starship – alone. But just being eccentric and a doubter would hardly justify the prodigious concentration of effort to prevent his trip. The unteleported man suspected he was on the track of a secret too dangerous to get out – even after an eighteen-year journey.

CLIFFORD D. SIMAK

Way Station

The inhabitants of the alien planets had many benefits to offer Earth – and were willing to share them if only Earth society showed signs of becoming adequately civilized.
As the only Earthman in touch with the rest of the universe, the keeper of Way Station 18327 was beginning to hope that his fellow men might at last prove worthy. Then his plans started to go wrong – starting with a grave robbery and ending on the night an ignorant and violent mob threatened to penetrate the innermost secrets of the Way Station . . .

JOHN BRUNNER

The Wrong End of Time

America in the future is a fortress ruled by fear. Through its massive defence works is smuggled a young Russian with a terrifying message. An alien ship has entered the solar system. Its threat – to boil the Earth's entire mass into raw energy!
'Alarming and persuasive' – *The Times*

Traveller in Black

The time was the unguessably remote past – or perhaps the distant future. Throughout the universe, Chaos ruled. Scientific laws of cause and effect held no force; men could not know from one day to the next what to expect from their labours, and even hope seemed foolish. In this universe there was one man to whom had been entrusted the task of bringing reason and order out of Chaos. He was a quiet man dressed in black who carried a staff made of light, and wherever he went the powers of Chaos swirled around him, buffeted him, tested him. He fought them, and little by little he drove them back. But the Traveller in Black himself belonged to the anti-science universe. If he succeeded in his task of changing the order of the cosmos, could he continue to live?

DAMON KNIGHT

Off Centre

Eight brilliantly inventive gems of science fiction by Damon Knight.

MEET:

Michael Kronski, an ordinary human being who can bend the past to his will
Pete the Dolphin who learns to talk to man
Kip Morgan who finds his body invaded by little blue men
The Martian who comes to visit Earth
God's Nose
Dulcie and Decorum

In Deep

Take a step forward and fall suddenly into a creeping blob of protoplasm, then discover that your three companions have fallen with you and your bodies have been digested by the 'Thing'.
Watch a man searching on a beach, and feel your blood run cold when he tells you what he is searching for.
A doorway that will take you anywhere – except back to Earth.
In Deep is a bizarre and brilliant volume of stories from the imagination of Damon Knight.